PEARLS OF SPIRITUAL WISDOM

by

Dr Aparna Chattopadhyay

Pustak Mahal®

J-3/16 , Daryaganj, New Delhi-110002
☎ 23276539, 23272783, 23272784 • *Fax:* 011-23260518
E-mail: info@pustakmahal.com • *Website:* www.pustakmahal.com

Sales Centre

- 10-B, Netaji Subhash Marg, Daryaganj, New Delhi-110002
  ☎ 23268292, 23268293, 23279900 • *Fax:* 011-23280567
  E-mail: rapidexdelhi@indiatimes.com
- **Hind Pustak Bhawan**
  6686, Khari Baoli, Delhi-110006
  ☎ 23944314, 23911979

Branches

Bengaluru: ☎ 080-22234025 • *Telefax:* 080-22240209
E-mail: pustak@airtelmail.in • pustak@sancharnet.in
Mumbai: ☎ 022-22010941, 022-22053387
E-mail: rapidex@bom5.vsnl.net.in
Patna: ☎ 0612-3294193 • *Telefax:* 0612-2302719
E-mail: rapidexptn@rediffmail.com
Hyderabad: *Telefax:* 040-24737290
E-mail: pustakmahalhyd@yahoo.co.in

ISBN 978-81-223-0858-9

Edition: 2011

Printed at : Unique Colour Cartoon, Delhi

My Prayer

O Lord, whether anyone around me does
the right thing or not,
becomes spiritual or not,
expresses love or not,
should not concern me.
Just let me do so....

Once you start on the spiritual journey,
you can never really get out of it.
It will not allow you to...

A little tolerance expressed daily will reward you
with peace, friendship and spiritual growth.

—Vikas Malkani

Prologue

In the wee hours of a freezing January, as I gazed out of the guesthouse window, a thick pall of mist hung over the blue-green hills of the sacred Vaishno Devi shrine. The snow-white shrine complex (*Bhavan*) seemed mystical amidst the floating clouds – almost like a magician's paradise straight out of a fairytale.

The haunting valleys and towering mountains dotted with whispering pine trees held an out-of-the-world mystic charm about them. The milky-white *Bhavan* would be visible one moment and suddenly disappear the next moment in the floating mist. The intriguing beauty of the view made me feel as though my very being was undergoing an electrifying rejuvenation.

Overwhelmed by the sanctity of the very air I breathed, I bowed my head in deep reverence and surrender to the Supreme Creator. The song of the chirping morning birds and the distant bells in the valley seemed like a divine greeting on that first day of the New Year... The cherished memory of those moments warms my heart even today.

In those magic moments, something within urged me to pen my divine experience and give free reign to my spiritual longings. I felt my very being experiencing a strange rejuvenation and empowerment. A compelling thought told me that the sooner I undertook this spiritual endeavour, the more tranquil would I feel. The longer I waited, the more would I be vulnerable to procrastination and, later, regret. So I earnestly decided to bring this venture of mine to you at the earliest.

The divine intricacies of our everyday life are amazingly inspiring indeed. They fill us with sheer gratefulness towards our Supreme Creator. Try and hear the symphony of His silence... In a million shades of His green universe, the blooming lilies, the smiling lotuses, the dancing butterflies, the whispering breezes, the cascading waterfalls, the chirping birds, the playful squirrels... The list is endless.

And suddenly, the realisation of a defining moment dawns upon you – inspiring you to delve deep into the subtle intricacies of life. Listen to that inner voice of yours to look beyond the immediate... You are here with a purpose. This life has not been given to you merely for the sake of making a livelihood but to endow it with the meaning it deserves. Listen to your inner voice, your inner call, for a greater vision of tomorrow, both for yourself and for the world around you. Take the road less travelled. Contemplate and introspect.

Once you do that, returning to the mundane world would seem impossible for you... not even the vast treasuries of this material kingdom would tempt you. For then, you shall have reached a state where nothing more is left to be known or felt...

—Dr Aparna Chattopadhyay

Contents

Prologue 5
Who are you? 9
What is your true Self? 11
Why are you here? 12
What is life? 14
You are unique 15
Living in spirituality 17
How do you relate to God? 19
Do you live and long for God? 21
Is your mind calm and restful? 23
Do you wish to live in the Now? 26
The art of mindful living 28
Heal yourself and heal the world 30
Do you wish to get rid of your ego? 32
Do you culture your thoughts? 34
Do you aspire for peace and happiness? 36
'This too shall pass' 40
Don't quit 43
Do you lead a detached life? 44
Are you at peace with yourself? 47
Do you perform daily activities in the right spirit? 49
At the day's end 51
Do you love God purely? 52
Are you centred outside your Self? 56
Are you a Karma Yogi? 60
Are you childlike? 63
Did you knock at the door of God? 65
Do you know the art of true prayer? 66
Others 68
Do you wish to cross the worldly ocean? 69

Is there life beyond death?	71
Use the Eight Magic Words to transform your life	73
Your desires and your destiny	75
Do you wish to reap the Divine Harvest?	77
The promise of God	79
Do you see the Divine in everything?	80
His precious gifts to you	82
The power of autosuggestion	86
Do you trust yourself?	89
Love – the nectar of life	90
Giving	93
Are you aware of your focus in life?	95
Meditation and the Self within	98
Do you have faith in God?	105
Footprints	108
Seek God when still young	109
Are you compassionate and unattached?	114
Acceptance	117
Do you possess a balanced mind?	118
Would you opt for the road less travelled?	120
Can you take personal control of your life?	122
Desires	124
Spirituality at work	126
Do you keep your cup empty when praying?	129
The spiritual Guru	131
Why should you have a Guru?	135
Service to Mankind	138
Harmony in Nature	140
Can you cope with destructive criticism?	142
Is compassion a way of life with you?	144
Is your education really complete?	149
Do you suffer death anxiety?	152
The homecoming	156
If I can	158

Who are you?

Eternal, unborn in the Self
Which is called the soul when it abides
In finite centres, bodies, forms,
In truth it is the Self of all.

Uncleaved, unwetted and unburnt,
Unwithered is the Source of all.
Glory immortal, Omnipotent,
Omnipresent and Omniscient.
–Bhagavad Gita II 23,24

Have you ever yearned to know your real nature and become aware of your basic truth? Because you have taken residence in this body, can you call it "I"? The "I" in you is like the tiny wave that plays with the wind for a moment, over the deep waters of the sea. Just as the wave appears to be separate from the sea, but you know that it is an inseparable part of the timeless ocean, similarly you too are not just the body, but a soul, which is a spark of the Almighty Creator.

Your body is just a vehicle for your soul. When you move about in a tonga (horse cart), do you say the tonga is you? You do not take the tonga inside when you step down from it on reaching home. So you have to drop this body of yours too when you reach your ultimate "home".

"Long identification with the material world has trained you that the false is true, that the temporary is eternal. You have to re-educate yourself into the right vision," says Sathya Sai Baba.

"The truest thing," Baba maintains, "the fact that persists unchanged is the 'I' itself – the *Atman.* All else is unreal but appears real."

Spend some time in silence everyday. Ask yourself the questions again and again: 'Who am I? Whence have I come? Where is my true home? Why am I here?'

One day the answer will come to you from the depths within. And to you will be revealed the secret of life...

OO

What is your true Self?

No soul is born, no soul does die,
Embodiments get remodelled,
Since evolution is the name
of advancement towards True Selfhood.
–Bhagavad Gita II.20

The Self is the universal absolute. You were the Self before birth and shall be the Self again after this sojourn on earth. Just as water which is clear and transparent sometimes gets muddy, but if you filter all the mud out it again comes to its original state, so does your consciousness get covered with the dust of your age-old mental conditioning.

Hence, to recognise your true Self, you must eliminate the false first – i.e., unlearn your identification with your body, emotions, thoughts etc. The sum total of your past thoughts, experiences, upbringing and genetic inheritance have created the likes, dislikes, interests, talents, habits and attitudes that you falsely believe is you.

Throughout your life's journey, although your body changes from a child's to an adult's, nevertheless, you still feel that you have a constant *identity*. You realise that though your body has undergone changes, yet your identity remains unchanged. In like manner, when your present body dies to be born again, your spirit remains unchanged. As Lord Krishna states in the *Bhagavad Gita*: "For the soul, there is never birth or death. It is unborn, eternal, ever existing, undying and primeval. It is not slain when the body is slain." This is your true self. Do not undermine it.

ᴐᴐ

Why are you here?

You are a child of the universe,
No less than the trees and the stars,
You have a right to be here...
Amidst the noisy confusion of life,
Keep inner peace with your soul.

With all its sham, drudgery and broken dreams,
It's still a beautiful world...
Old Saint Paul's Church, Baltimore 1692

What is so unique about having a human physical body? The body of man is necessary because it is able to reveal the unseen God, the indwelling divinity.

"Most of us," says Sathya Sai Baba, "are unaware that the divine force is as much as 80 per cent present in the human form and it is thus unique in this respect. Human life is sacred and must be appreciated as having the highest value. In the animal, only about 15 per cent is present. Man can raise himself to union with God, whereas the animal can never be free of its natural state."

For example, the tiger cannot be trained to eat food made from grains because his *impulse* is to kill and eat offal (remains). In the case of a human being, he has the *wisdom* to understand and make a distinction between the righteous and unrighteous path.

Human birth is a special opportunity to attain freedom from the cycle of birth and death and only through human birth may God be realised. Here and now is the individual.

Here and now is the golden opportunity to realise the absolute goal of life, for who can be sure of the conditions and status of his next birth? This great *life secret* should be understood by one and all and even five minutes of time wasted is a tragic loss in the face of the magnificence of this rare human opportunity.

When you become aware that you are a spark of the ever pervading, omniscient and omnipotent Almighty Creator, you will feel linked with all animate and inanimate entities who are also sparks of the same Creator. You will then rise above your ego and a sudden realisation will dawn upon you that all are equal, irrespective of caste and creed, and are manifestations of the same cosmic power.

This leads to the ultimate question: Why are we here? The answer is – to help each other. Help as many as you can to lift the load on the rough road of life and remember: He helps those who help others.

OO

What is life?

Life is a mixture of sunshine and rain,
Laughter and pleasure, teardrops and pain.
All days can't be bright, but it's certainly true,
There was never a
cloud the sun didn't shine through.

So just keep on smiling whatever betide you,
Secure in the knowledge God is always beside you.

And you'll find when you smile,
Your day will be brighter.
And all of your burdens will seem so much lighter –
For each time you smile you will find it true,
Somebody, somewhere will smile back at you.

And nothing on earth can make life more worthwhile
Than the sunshine and warmth of a beautiful smile.

–Helen Steiner Rice

OO

You are unique

Do all the good you can,
By all the means you can,
In all the ways you can,
In all the places you can,
At all the times you can,
To all the people you can,
As long as you can.
–John Wesley

Are you aware of your blessedness? "The key to blessedness lies in being aware of your blessedness," says Swami Chidananda. If you turn your awareness in different directions, towards what you do not have, or what you think or imagine you do not have, then this wrongly directed pattern of thought would make you unaware of the many things that you have.

You are unique and distinct in the eyes of the Creator. There is none like you, as a particular being. Each one is precious and especially valuable to the Creator. No one can replace you in the role that you fulfil in God's creation at any given place and at any given point of time. You are most necessary and indispensable for that particular set-up, in that particular time-space context. Therefore, rejoice and be grateful to the Lord that He has given you a role to perform.

Remember that the role He gives you to perform is in accordance with your capability and thus God expects each one to do what one is capable of, at any point, at any time. Surely, God does not expect an ant to haul loads of timber, as the elephant does in the forest. Nor does God expect the elephant to fly gracefully in the air, as do swallows and doves. He expects the birds to fly and He loves them for what they do. And He expects man to live as man. Each one in his own place, in his own sphere, can fulfil a task and gladden the heart of the Maker and contribute something to His plan on earth.

This is the truth. And to be aware of the truth is to be worry-free, anxiety-free. To be aware of the truth is to be grateful to God and express your gratefulness thus: "You have made me unique. You have given me a role, and you have prompted me and brought me all helpful factors to fulfil my role and play my part. For that I ever give my thanks to you."

So rejoice in the serene calmness of spirit: "I have arrived, I am in the presence of God and I am totally accepted. I have a special and unique place in God's heart." God's infinite heart is large enough to hold the entire cosmos and everything within it.

Thus knowing, have great comfort in your heart, great satisfaction and contentment. And that is the secret of inner joy, the key of blessedness and the pathway to peace, serenity and inner calm, where there is no fretting, agitation or restlessness. Rejoice that He is not a remote reality, but He is the indwelling Reality, nearer to you than anything else on earth. For within you is the peace of God as your own self.

"You are God's peace and you have a duty to perform, that is, to spread this peace which you are, to one and all. Live to spread this peace," says Swami Chidananda.

OO

Living in spirituality

Who views the One in friend and foe,
Dishonour, honour, heat and cold.
In pleasure, pain, censure and praise,
Silent and content with what comes.

Homeless, and rooted in one's aim,
That blessed one hails excellent.
On earth as also in heaven,
Is loved by God as best of men.

–Bhagavad Gita XII.13,19

"I often say, religion is the banana skin and spirituality is the banana. The misery in the world is because we throw away the banana and we are holding on to the dry skin. So, we need to enhance the spiritual aspect of our life," says Sri Sri Ravi Shankar.

Your awareness of your intrinsic link with the universe and its living beings and seeing the presence of your Creator in them enables you to get in touch with spirituality. Faith dawns upon you and this faith in the Creator accelerates your love for everyone – this is the blueprint of living in spirituality and of the Life Divine – which each one of us has the potential to realise.

And when we learn to connect with the tranquil, small voice within us, and listen to the prompting of our inner guru, we see our own deepest Self in others and realise that all are intrinsically divine.

"People feel that by going to temples and purely by performing religious rites they can attain communion with God. But spirituality truly lies in being devoted to one's duty, one's work, to be content and above all, being true to yourself and all other people who have faith in you. One who has the courage to be honest and positive under adverse circumstances is truly spiritual," says Padma Bhushan and Sahitya Kala Academy Award winner music maestro Jagjit Singh.

OO

How do you relate to God?

Lo! Transient is the world of pain,
Attach thyself to nothing here,
For fleeting shadows are these forms
Which look like beauties and treasures.

With mind and soul in rooted pose,
In concentrated communion
Who rests ever on the lap of God
Such soul attains God alone.

–Bhagavad Gita IX.33,34

Just as you raise a rose-creeper by nurturing it tenderly and lovingly and one day it bears beautiful fragrant roses for you, likewise if you protect and nurture the tender creeper of your Self in devotional service sincerely, it will gradually produce the fruit of unalloyed love for God – love that is neither tinged by desire for worldly and material benefits, for mere philosophical understanding, nor for fruitful results.

Unalloyed love is to know that "God is great, I'm His part and parcel, and therefore He is my supreme lovable object". This consciousness is the highest perfection of human life and the ultimate aim of all methods of self-realisation. When one reaches this point – God is my only beloved – then one's life is perfect and meaningful. Tasting that transcendental relationship with one's Creator gives real happiness.

When you bask in the winter Sun, does the Sun ask you for anything in return? When you rest awhile under a shady tree on a scorching summer afternoon, does the tree expect any favour from you in return for its service? But when you worship God, do you worship Him with such a spirit? If one has material desires or motives within him and for the fulfilment of such desires, engages himself in devotional service, the result is that he will not receive the pure love of God.

Pure devotion is devoid of all desires – it is simply to render loving service for its own sake. Without a motive, without desire for personal sense gratification, service should be rendered to the Supreme Lord and His devotees.

OO

Do you live and long for God?

This Supreme Person, Power and Bliss,
Is reached with love that wants none else.
The ardour surging from the soul,
Tearing the veils of involvement.

Through whole-souled love and devotion
Can one attain this blessedness.
By utter sinking of the Self,
In All-Self, greatest Almighty.

–Bhagavad Gita VIII.21,22

The prayer of the enlightened is the prayer that is full of love. It is the ocean full of movement, but with nowhere to go. It is self-contained.

The divine experience comes with a natural inevitability to the sincere devotee. His intense craving begins to pull at God with an irresistible force. The Lord as the Cosmic Vision is drawn by the magnetic ardour of the seeker's elevated consciousness. He realises that it is the spirit of God that actively sustains every form and force in the universe. The joys of life are illusory, and so are the pains of life, as both are just reactions caused by the changing phases of life.

Most of us think ourselves to be religious and God-conscious, but do we really love God in the true sense? When you are actually on the platform of love for God, you understand your relationship with God as: "I am a part and parcel of God."

Thus, you unconsciously extend your love to the other living beings too – animals, birds, and insects. If you actually love God, your love extends to all living beings, animate and inanimate. You logically analyse: "This insect has a different body but he is also a part and parcel of my Creator."

When you think in this way, you cannot maintain a slaughterhouse. "If you maintain a slaughterhouse and disobey the order of Christ, 'Thou shalt not kill' and you proclaim yourself to be a Christian or a Hindu, that is not religion," says Swami Sivananda, the founder of Divine Life Society.

We may be Hindus, Christians, Muslims or Sikhs, but does it mean God is Hindu, Christian, Muslim or Sikh? True religion is the worship of a universal Supreme Power – God. To love and remember God, make this your daily prayer:

With the heart enshrined
In the secret of Name,
The Name Divine –
The way to unlock the secret
Is the way of Love!
Teach me, O Lord,
To Love thee,
Not myself!
So bless me that forsaking myself
I may think of Thy Lotus-feet
By day and by night!

As described in the *Bhagavad Gita* (VIII.21,22), the following modes of attitude are to be borne in mind to realise and love God:

This Supreme Person, Power and Bliss
Is reached with Love that wants none else,
The ardour surging from the soul,
Tearing the veils of involvement.
Through whole-souled love and devotion
Can one attain this blessedness!
By utter sinking of the Self
In All-Self, greatest Almighty.

OO

Is your mind calm and restful?

There is something in you which is immortal, indestructible, eternal. The ego makes you a coward... Bring out your Buddha as a fully-opened lotus in the early morning Sun, with small dew-drops shining beautifully... This egolessness makes you a fearless pilgrim of the eternal mystery of life.
–Osho's commentary on a sutra by Ta Hui. Chapter 28 of Osho's book, *The Great Zen Master Ta Hui*.

The cosmic vision leaves many permanent lessons. By daily stilling of your thoughts, you can be released from the delusive conviction that the body is a mass of flesh and bones, traversing the hard soil of matter. The breath and the restless, ever-chattering mind are like storms that leash the ocean of light into waves of material forms – earth, sky, human beings, animals, birds, and trees. Only by calming these storms can one have the perception of the Infinite as One Light.

Scientific studies suggest connections between the body and mind, implying that emotional state and thought processes affect the brain, endocrine system and also the immune system. So when your mind is not calm but tense, you are automatically more vulnerable and prone to disease. A new discipline has emerged based on these concepts – psychoneuro-immunology or mind-body medicine.

The perception of stress leads to restlessness, anxiety, irritability or aggressive behaviour and/or a state of panic. In extreme cases, it even leads to addiction to tobacco, alcohol or drugs. Negative emotions surface in the form of hatred, dislike, jealousy, greed, possessiveness, lust, arrogance and anger.

Furthermore, interpersonal relationships are adversely affected, the work output decreases and concentration wanes. Efficiency diminishes and the memory weakens. Most of us are afraid to acknowledge our negativity and begin finding fault with others. We start complaining, which further adds to our stress and a vicious cycle begins.

Exposure or perception of repeated stressful situations (chronic stress) leads to irrevocable physiological changes, resulting in diseased states like high blood pressure, diabetes, heart attack, asthma, viral infections, gastrointestinal ulcers, migraine and non-specific headaches etc.

How should one then counter stress? Over the centuries, many sages and saints have recommended the practice of Yoga, meditation and Pranayam to prevent or alter our reaction to stress. More recently, Sri Sri Ravi Shankar – founder of the Art of Living course – has introduced Sudarshan Kriya (a rhythmic breathing process). These are processes that not only affect the mind and body, but also take it beyond, towards the very source of our body-mind and emotion consciousness.

According to Sri Sri Ravi Shankar: "Breath and mind are linked like body and mind. Breath sorts out the imbalances in the body and the mind. It's the secret of life which we have forgotten."

Pranayam is an ancient wisdom. It directs or regulates our *prana* – subtle life-force energy, the very essence of our life. Regular practice of Pranayam activates and harmonises many biological rhythms, including the brain rhythm, heartbeat, enzyme rhythm and the mental and emotional rhythm.

Often, stress is perceived only when our consciousness is flowing outwards, when our mind, senses and emotions are connected to the outside world, to the environment and to the events of life. But when our consciousness is turned inwards, when the senses, thoughts and emotions are harmonised with consciousness, we experience a "state of Pure Consciousness", where there is no stress, and one perceives only joy. One has to experience and realise this state for it to affect a change at the level of our psyche, thoughts, emotions and body.

One has to thus enter into the state of relaxed alertness, where there is a considerable increase in the alpha activity of one's brain, whereby the body feels younger and healthier, emotions are more balanced, and the mind feels calmer.

OO

Do you wish to live in the Now?

Let go of all impressions...
Be hollow and empty.
Think fresh and feel free.
–Sri Sri Ravi Shankar

Strangely enough, most of us tend not to live in the present. Let us always remind ourselves that neither the past nor the future exist – we only live in the present – the Now. By transcending the mind's compulsive tendency to live in the past and the future, we can live fully, intensely, and enjoy the bliss of enlightenment. Accepting every moment as it unfolds, no matter what it contains, is the art of living in the Now.

The eternal present is the space within which your whole life unfolds the one factor that remains constant – life is Now. There was never a time when your life was not Now, nor will there be. The Now is a consequence of our past and it will determine the quality of our future life. Hence, the present moment holds the grave of the past and the seed of the future. So do not deliver your life in 'what was' or 'what will be'. Live life in 'what is'.

"Seek to cultivate a condition where you are no longer frightened by the complexity of life, but indeed are thrilled by the challenge of trying to truly understand it," says Andrew Cohen, spiritual teacher and founder of *What is Enlightenment?* magazine.

"Look beyond the events, dissolve into infinity, and be in the moment," says Sri Sri Ravi Shankar. Remember that everything is temporary; everything is changing. Yesterday is gone; tomorrow may never come – so live your life today.

OO

The art of mindful living

The Sun rises and celebrates,
The sky embraces and celebrates.
Winds blow and celebrate,
Rivers flow and celebrate.
Birds sing and celebrate,
Peacocks dance and celebrate.
Trees flower and celebrate,
Buds bloom and celebrate.
We smile and serve,
Meditate and celebrate.
–Sri Sri Ravi Shankar

You can make a spiritual practice of watching every thought, every action, every feeling. Each time your mind drifts away, try to bring it back. Invest time and energy in being *mindful* of each moment. Examine the contents of your mind *without judgement* or preference, thereby witnessing your action dispassionately.

Thus you can learn to celebrate the mundane by being in the moment. In this way, even ordinary chores that you have to perform shall no more appear ordinary to you.

When you observe your thoughts dispassionately, your negative emotions such as anger, gloom, depression, jealousy etc lose their very power and get diluted. Awareness of your negative emotions thus helps in dealing with them.

If you are able to recognise the moment when anger arises, you will be able to distinguish the part of your mind that is feeling the anger. This will divide your mind into two parts – one part will be feeling anger while the other will be trying to observe. Therefore, anger cannot dominate the entire mind. You are able to recognise that anger is harmful and maybe develop an antidote to it. View your anger objectively. Try to see the positive side of the anger-causing person or event.

OO

Heal yourself and heal the world

My body may be sick and
my physical heart may not function properly,
yet within my soul –
the spiritual heart dwells,
the spirit of God who ever healeth and blesseth!
Each day, this spirit is renewing
my body, my mind, my heart.
And I feel strong and radiant
and serenely happy.

–JP Vaswani

Just as you need to switch on your computer and connect to the Internet, in like manner you need to connect to your original source, your Supreme Powerhouse – the Almighty. This connectivity can be attained through meditation, wherein you rise above your physical body and centre around your astral or mind body, which takes you nearer to God. Meditation thus heals your inner being and touches your day-to-day life. Nowadays, even in hospitals doctors have begun meditation classes for quicker healing of patients.

The latest medical research shows that while there are 12 to 20 cycles of brain waves per second during normal daily life, during meditation this comes down to only 4 to 8 cycles per second and even lower, as we reach the alpha, theta and delta states in which the mind is completely calm, composed and relaxed. This slowdown in the brain-waves process ensures a calming and stilling of our mind, allowing us to connect with our Original Self. We then become less reactive and less driven by our instincts, impulses and desires.

Thereby, we are more peaceful, centred and harmonious. We are able to heal the inner child within us through meditation. And if each one heals one's own Self through meditation and concentrates on the Higher Self, world healing automatically takes place.

Psychological research reveals that an inner child dwells within each one of us. When we are deprived of love in our childhood, our inner child craves for love and affection and becomes fixated on love. So even though we attain physical maturity, we react to frustration and adversities in a childish manner by raising our voice or acting stubborn and cranky. But as we meditate and gradually get closer to God, feeling His love, it heals the deprived inner child within us and our responses thus become full of calm and serenity.

In this manner, we prevent various psychosomatic diseases such as heart ailments, digestive problems, depression etc. A healed healthy body and mind for each one thus builds a stronger, healthier nation and a healthier world.

OO

Do you wish to get rid of your ego?

If you possess an ability that others do not, do not let it go to your head. Remember that it was God who chose to give you that ability over others.
–Vikas Malkani

Egoism is the most dangerous weakness of Man. It leads to the downfall of the spiritual aspirant. On account of egoism, one considers himself the *doer.* Egoism blocks the full flow of the Divine Energy. "Ego is a steel wall that separates Man from the Lord," says Swami Sivananda. Wherever there is ego, there is selfishness, likes and dislikes, hypocrisy and the idea of doership. An egoist wants to exercise power and influence over others, and feels superior to others. At times, even *yogis* are not free from the ego of their *siddhis.* The real devotee is one who is free from this evil trait through the grace of God.

To get rid of the ego, study it dispassionately. One has to introspect, develop self-awareness and remove vanity consciously by becoming aware of one's shortcomings. Having constant *satsang* (company of the spiritually enlightened) and being steeped in love with the Divine shall free us from our ego.

In the words of Sathya Sai Baba: "God dwells in you as joy. That is why you seek joy always in every object around you. To become as full of joy as Radha or Ramakrishna, or Vivekananda, you have to sacrifice your ego, and saturate yourself with the Lord, with the consciousness that the Lord is your being. So long as you have a trace of ego in you, you cannot see the Lord clearly."

Baba further explains: "Egoism will be destroyed if you constantly tell yourself: 'It is He, not I. He is the force; I am but the instrument.' Keep His name always on the tongue; contemplate His glory whenever you hear or see anything beautiful or grand; see in everyone the Lord Himself, moving in that form. Do not speak evil of others; see only the good in them. Welcome every chance to help others, to console them, to encourage them along the spiritual path. Be humble! Do not become proud of your wealth or status or authority, learning and class. Dedicate all your physical possessions and mental skills and intellectual attainments to the service of the Lord. Then your ego will be wiped out."

○○

Do you culture your thoughts?

Two men look through the prison bars.
One sees the mud, the other – the stars.
–Denis Robins, One Sees Stars

Your thoughts are the architect of your destiny. The human mind is like a wireless machine. A positive mind emits harmonious waves of thoughts, which travel with lightning speed and echo in the minds of others. In contrast, a negative mind sends out discordant thoughts.

Thoughts can heal and change mindsets. If you learn the art of thought culture, you can tap thought power for leading a dynamic and positive life. Swami Sivananda, founder of the Divine Life Society of India, contends that the mind being a centre of supernormal powers commands higher faculties for thought transcendence leading Man into the domains of divine realisation.

You can culture your thoughts just as one cultures a pearl. Thought is both force and motion. It is dynamic. Very few people know the art of thought culture. Every one of us has his own mental world, his own mode of thinking. Negative thoughts such as hatred, lust, jealousy and selfishness produce distorted images in the mind and cause clouding of understanding, perversion of intellect, loss of memory and confusion.

Every thought has an image, form, dimension, weight, shape, colour etc. Thought is as much matter as a piece of stone. Thoughts move and pass from one individual to another. A man of powerful thoughts can readily influence people of weak thoughts. We should develop the faculty of producing only pure *Sattvik* thoughts by protracted mental discipline, diet adjustments, and repetition of spiritual mantras with meaning, study of divine books, meditation and prayer.

A good man can help his friend, even though he lives a long distance away, by sending him good thoughts. We must not allow evil thoughts to enter our minds. We must always watch our thoughts. Avoid useless and base thinking and conserve mental energy, as energy is wasted in idle thinking and chattering of the mind.

We can thereby cultivate good and sublime thoughts and feed affirmative ones to our programmed mind, thus pruning away negative thoughts, just as the gardener prunes the rose plant to grow beautiful blossoms.

OO

Do you aspire for peace and happiness?

Happiness is a sunbeam which may pass through a thousand bosoms without losing a particle of its original ray; nay, when it strikes on a kindred heart, like the converged light on a mirror, it reflects itself with redoubled brightness. It is not perfected till it is shared.

–Jane Porter

"The gateway to a happy life is through your heart, not through your mind," says spiritual guru Vikas Malkani. Nurture your heart with spirituality. It is difficult to experience peace and happiness without giving spirituality a prominent place in life. Man has air-conditioned cars, houses and offices but he still does not enjoy peace of mind.

Caught as he is in the whirlpool of materialistic miasma, modern man has been seeking joy through sensual aggrandisement, which unfortunately turns out to be a short-lived affair and a painful experience at times. The restlessness and tensions of the mind overpower him to the extent that some people commit suicide even while living in affluent homes. Obviously, peace and happiness do not reside in external objects but within us. It is of an elusive quality and can be experienced only when we give it to others.

Happiness is a subjective phenomenon. Our happiness depends on how we perceive and view our circumstances rather than what they actually are. Two men look through the prison bars and one sees the mud, the other, the stars. To quote Abraham Lincoln, "Most folks are about as happy as they make up their minds to be."

Thus some people blessed with material comforts may remain cynical because they haven't achieved their goals, while despite a serious illness and limited income, others may be happier because of a more positive outlook. In fact, in a poll across 18 nations on the issue of happiness, the Icelanders – living on a windswept island, surrounded by glaciers and volcanoes – were discovered to be the happiest people!

"Often, we are unhappy not because life is causing unhappiness, but because of our opinion of how life should be," says Swami Sukhabodhananda. The state of highest happiness is that in which the consciousness is universal, free as the air, and can identify itself with every passing movement, the flight of a bird, the quivering leaf, the care of an ant, the smiles and tears of other human beings – all in an instant.

Spirituality is the science that teaches us how to free and uncondition our minds. As maintained by Swami Ramakrishna Paramahansa, spirituality is virtually as enriching for your life as adding the figure 1 to many zeros. If you add one to six zeros it multiplies to become a million. And without the one, the zeros have no identity at all! Likewise, spirituality is to our lives what 1 is to these zeros. One who has integrated spiritual ideals into his life can be peaceful and happy under any circumstance or situation. We have to perfect the art and science of looking within for joy and happiness that is everlasting, sans any trace of pain and sorrow.

No one can give happiness to another. We shall come closer to finding inner happiness and contentment if we do not think of our spiritual life and our practical life as existing without connection. These two realms, the practical and the spiritual, are interconnected rooms in the house of life. The door must be kept open between them. Remember the beautiful couplet in the words of Swami Sukhabodhananda: "We touch the earth using the physical foot, we touch life using the psychological foot."

In the *Bhagavad Gita*, Lord Krishna tells Arjuna: "He who enjoys the happiness of the Self, does not care for any power." Thus graduating from sensual life to spiritual life should be our aim.

"Physical strength can never permanently withstand the impact of spiritual force," said Franklin Roosevelt.

The truth is that, if a man puts himself in accord with the divine law, happiness results from such harmony. The error is to identify worldly success with happiness and to disregard the element of time.

The more man progresses, the more elevated and enlightened will be his consciousness. Happiness, indeed, may be called a characteristic of progress. In the course of its development it becomes more and more sublime, until it grows into that serenity which radiates from the face of the Enlightened One with that subtle smile in which wisdom, compassion, and all-embracing love are mingled.

There is but one way to tranquillity of mind and happiness; therefore, let this always be ready at hand with you, both when you wake up early in the morning and all day long, and when you go late to sleep and to account for no external things as your own, but to commit all those to God.

Most often, our expectations determine our state of happiness. The more we expect and the more we compare ourselves with others who seem better off, the more frustrated and unhappy we become. In fact, happiness lies in achieving a balance between expectations and achievements. The more we reduce our expectations, the happier we become.

Behavioural psychologist Diener discovered that happy people tend to have higher self-esteem, satisfying relationships with others, are socially outgoing, employed, exercise regularly and sleep well. But what appears to be most important for adult happiness is the certainty that life has meaning and direction.

Both happiness and sorrow are created by the mind. We can only experience real peace and bliss when the pendulum of the mind stops swinging from happiness to sorrow alternatively. This state of perfect stillness is verily the essence of life.

As the mystic Jnaneshwar says: "He who does not return to the world of senses from his life in *Atman*, there is no wonder that such a man should cease to care for sensual enjoyment."

OO

'This too shall pass'

Fixing thy mind on Me, thou shalt by My grace, overcome all obstacles; but if from egoism thou wilt not hear Me, thou shalt perish.

–Bhagavad Gita XVIII.58

"The sugarcane should welcome the cutting, the hacking and the crushing it is subjected to. Without these ordeals, the cane would dry up and make no tongue sweet. So too, man must welcome trouble, for that alone brings sweetness to the spirit within," says Sathya Sai Baba. In times of adversity and distress, remember and repeat one mantra to yourself – 'This too shall pass'.

As the sunrise is followed by the sunset and vice versa, so does the pendulum of joy and sorrow swing alternately throughout our lifespan. When you meet sorrow, rest assured and repeat to yourself: "This too shall pass", as it is also evanescent like all other things and phases of life.

Shape your mental attitude to ignore the negative aspects of your ailment. When a child falls while playing in the garden, the mother tries to divert his attention by exclaiming to him: "Oh! See the beautiful sparrow on the tree." Or, "Oh! That's a colourful butterfly on the flower!" Thus, the child's attention is diverted and he gets engrossed in admiring the sparrow or the butterfly and forgets his trouble.

In like manner, do not take your moments of adversity too seriously and instead try to divert your attention away from it towards more positive spheres, with a positive philosophy of life.

Prayer is a powerful positive influence on one's mind, body and spirit. Remember that prayer can achieve more things than we believe. Sincere prayer, *japa* (chanting) of Aum or any other devotional mantra, divine grace, or the grace of the guru can overcome any kinds of calamities, illnesses and sorrows. Patanjali Maharishi prescribes *japa* or chanting of Aum with devotion and meaning for the removal of obstacles. In the *Bhagavad Gita* (Ch. XVIII), in His message Lord Krishna prescribes this remedy: "Fixing the thought on Me, thou shalt surmount every difficulty by My grace."

There is always a purpose and a cause behind man's suffering. When you suffer, it is the fruition of some old karmic debt of yours, which you have to pay off by undergoing that suffering. The law of harvest – *As you sow, so shall you reap* – is all-powerful. Your deeds can make you laugh or cry. Your share of give and take in the world as per your *karmas* will be completed by His grace. God is the ultimate performer of all your actions, as only He knows your past *karmas* and your give and take.

God is all merciful and benevolent and gives you pain only as a learning experience for your soul to illuminate. Your suffering is nothing but a stepping-stone for your soul's spiritual evolution. Just as gold attains its glow and glitter after being heated in the fire, so also the human being attains purification and spiritual maturity after paying off its karmic debt of innumerable past lives.

Contemplation of God with undaunted faith and reverence in Him, and accepting pain and sorrow as well as joy and happiness with equanimity and regarding them as His precious gifts is the right approach to treat the events of your life. As nothing happens without His will, accept even your pain and sorrow as His will and have faith in Him. The million-dollar mantra, 'This too shall pass' shall impart its powerful healing powers to you and to all your pains.

To quote Sathya Sai Baba: "Become aware of your reality and you will lose the sense of identification with the body.

That will make you disease-free and you will have perfect ease. Be ever in the consciousness that you are but a shadow of God – His image. Then no harm can hamper you. God walks along the Royal Road of Truth. The shadow holding to Him by the Feet falls on hollow and hill, fire and water, dirt and dust. But holding to the Feet as the shadow, you will be unaffected by the ups and downs of life."

OO

Don't quit

When things go wrong as they sometimes will,
When the road you're trudging seems all uphill,
When the funds are low and the debts are high,
And you want to smile, but you have to sigh,
When care is pressing you down a bit –
Rest, if you must, but don't quit.

Life is queer with its twists and turns,
As everyone of us sometimes learns,
And many a failure turns about,
When he might have won had he stuck it out;
Don't give up though the pace seems slow –
You may succeed with another blow!

Success is failure turned inside out –
The silver tint of the clouds of doubt,
And you never can tell how close you are,
It may be near when it seems so far;
So stick to the fight when you're hardest hit –
It's when things seem worst that you mustn't quit.

–Anonymous

OO

Do you lead a detached life?

O my soul! Living in this world of attractions and allurements, may you not for a single moment, forget the Home to which you have to return before nightfall!

Do not give your heart to this passing show. But, standing on the bank of the river, listen to the music of the falling waters and enjoy the beauty of the landscape.

Do not soil your feet with mud. And do not enter into the waters of Maya.

He who does not enter into the waters can never be drowned.

–JP Vaswani

If you wish to know the art of living with detachment, "live life like the posted note", says Jaya Row, the noted Vedantist, in her discourses. The posted note is a small bookmark which has some self-sticking adhesive. It is specially produced not to permanently stick to the page of your book or notes, so it comes out clean whenever you wish to remove it or stick it on another page.

A realised soul lives in the world with detachment. He is unattached and yet is dynamic and actively engaged in the world, because he does not stick to it and can come out of it clean and clear wherever he is. He realises the futility of getting stuck to the material world.

Most of us are like Fevicol, though! We get stuck fast to worldly attachments. We must remember that the mind is whimsical. It should be firmly under the control of the intellect.

This will lead to mental peace, and will, in turn, sharpen the intellect, and ultimately ensure happiness.

Renunciation does not mean retiring into a cave. It means letting go of the individual self to realise the Universal Self. A realised person moves about freely in the midst of worldly enticements, his mind absolutely unaffected by them. Sense control has nothing to do with the quantum of contact with sense objects, but about whether your intellect is in place and in charge. Always remember: Happiness = Number of desires actualised/number of desires harboured.

The best of us go through life trying to reduce our wants to attain contentment. But the secret lies in the denominator, the number of desires entertained. The smaller *that* is, the happier you are. And if it is down to zero, you have infinity. Forget the numerator and focus on the denominator.

Life is a dream. Take the example of your dream in the dream state. You have (a) a waking state of consciousness, (b) a dream state which is a totally different state, far removed from real life, and (c) you have a deep sleep state, in which you do not dream. When in the dream state, you may enjoy being rich, famous, and successful in the dream and get a thrill out of all that you experience. But once your dream is over and you get into the conscious state, you realise the futility of those dream experiences, which were unreal. But if you are given another chance to *relive* that dream of yours again in your waking state and acquire even more status and fame, say a Padma Vibhushan attached to your name, would you feel the *same* thrill again which you experienced in your dream? Obviously not! You know now that it holds no thrill, as it is *not real*. An enlightened person also feels the same way about the attractions of this ephemeral world. He gets no thrill out of them, as they are trivial and unreal to him, just like when you woke up from the dream into your conscious state.

Spiritual knowledge of Vedanta makes one aware of this eternal truth. It may look like the lightning and shock one in the beginning. But later on it becomes as natural as the blinking of our eye is to us. We see everything despite the blinking of our eye every second. In like manner, the vision of reality is uninterrupted and constant to a realised soul.

This sort of vision makes the realised soul truly detached and thus truly happy in the world. As a result of this, desires go, collateral benefits and success follow and happiness unfolds its invisible wings. Happiness that is so elusive and yet so much within one's inner self.

There is the story of a fly that was struggling miserably against the windowpane to set herself free and fly across the closed window. In her desperation, she tried harder and harder against the windowpane till she ultimately died. Little did she realise or see the open door, which was just two feet away from her!

Likewise, happiness too is just round the corner - you have only to look within to realise it. Becoming *antarmukhi* (looking within oneself) and detaching oneself from worldly attractions is all that is needed.

OO

Are you at peace with yourself?

Peace, true peace, is at the Lotus feet of the Lord.
And He is not afar. He is right where we are.
When we become conscious of His loving presence,
when we commune with Him, within the veil of silence,
we are filled with a sense of radiant joy and profound peace.
God's love enfolds us and we are never alone.
Blessed be His Name.
–JP Vaswani

Ask yourself whether peace is somewhere outside to be sought after! Or is it a commodity in the market to be purchased!! And most of all, how are we leading our lives? By cheating, falsehood, and passions such as anger, jealousy, hatred, selfishness etc? How can we ever enjoy peace then?

To enjoy peace of mind, we have to establish harmony within. Harmony within can be established by being at peace with one's inner self through meditating upon God.

In the *Bhagavad Gita*, Lord Krishna says: *"Rama yesha krodha yesha rajoguna samudbhuvah, Mahashano mahapapma vidyenamiha vairinam,"* meaning thereby that it is a sensual desire, anger born of great craving and sin; know this as the enemy here in human life. Anger can be controlled through pure love; miserliness through charity; jealousy through appreciation of talents or wealth and so on. Conscious practice of certain moral and spiritual values in life becomes a habit, and continuous habits mould the character. Once these spiritual values become our character, we acquire the secret of peaceful living and co-existence.

Just as a child feels at peace and secure after holding his mother's hand in a crowded marketplace, similarly, surrender your life totally at His feet and feel secure in the wilderness of this world. Know that you are the child of the omniscient and omnipotent God and are loved and looked after by Him. Do not try to burden yourself unnecessarily with endless worries and responsibilities. Remember, you are *not* the doer of your life's events.

There is an interesting story of a simpleton who was carrying a lot of luggage during a train journey. He suddenly put one of the big suitcases on his head while he stood in the crowded train. When someone asked him the reason for it, he retorted in a simple manner: "Well, the train is overloaded already and may not be able to bear the burden of my suitcase, so I am carrying it myself!" We might mock at Mr Simpleton, but are we not doing the same in our lives too? Seldom do we remind ourselves that we are *not* the sole decision-makers of our life's events.

As long as we remain agitated with life's worries and try to solve them alone, considering ourselves to be the doers, we act like Mr Simpleton in the train journey.

If only you delve deep within the recesses of your heart and be in communion with that Almighty power with complete faith in His grace, you would know what the bliss of inner peace is. And with His Grace unfolding and surrounding you, you would learn to rely on Him alone.... and turn to Him for all your needs. And you will lack nothing.

OO

Do you perform daily activities in the right spirit?

So bless me, Lord!
That I may learn the one and
only lesson I need to learn....
utter dependence on Thee and
dedicating every action unto Thee!
–JP Vaswani

As you go about performing your day's chores, dedicate every action, every routine chore unto the Lord, for His sake. The act is dedicated to the Lord and the results, therefore, are borne by the Lord. Actions done thus with the thoughts of fruits abandoned at the time of the action – such action is free of *karma.* In this way, since the ego is not fed and cultivated, it disappears before long.

Says Sathya Sai Baba: "If one shaves, which is classed as an uninspiring mundane task, the attitude is that one is preparing for the sake of the Lord in the heart, and one is making the best of his appearance to honour the Lord, and not for one's personal vanity or reward. Also, in walking, offer the action to the Lord to maintain a body fit for the Lord to live in; and see that this is the attitude for every single act of the day. Sweeping the house is dedicated to the Lord so that He may have a fit dwelling (inside your fit body). And may cooking also be dedicated to Him so that the body is strong and vigorous for the benefit of the Lord."

When one dies, the only possessions taken along are one's good and bad deeds. None of the power, the money, the position, the prestige, the beauty of the body, the culture of the personality remain – all are gone and, therefore, what a folly to work for them alone. They are not the end but the means towards the Godly end. "Man is life with desire; life without desire is God," says Sathya Sai Baba. Mind alone is desire; when mind disappears, desire too disappears.

But the difficulty arises when we devote all time in our life to activities which are only *means*; thinking them to be our *ends,* we seem to make them the *summum bonum* of our lives and forget the real purpose or goal of our life – God realisation. We need material possessions in life to enable ourselves to realise God through self-realisation and *not* for the sake of becoming masters of those worldly objects.

If we perform each activity of our day all through our life in this spirit, our whole life's activities would become a garland of flowers dedicated to the Lord.... in complete surrender.

OO

At the day's end

O Divine Master,
Grant that I may not seek so much
To be consoled as to console;
To be understood as to understand;
To be loved as to love;
For it is in giving that we receive,
It is in pardoning that we are pardoned;
And it is in dying to the little self
That we are born to eternal life.
–St Francis of Assisi

Ask yourself and introspect at the day's end:
Is anybody happier because you passed his way?
The day is almost over and its toiling is through;
Is there anyone to utter now a kindly word to you?

Does anyone remember that you spoke to him today?

Can you say tonight, in parting with the day that's slipping fast,
That you helped a single brother of the many that you passed?

Did you waste the day, or lose it?
Was it well or sorely spent?

Is a single heart rejoicing over what you did or said?
Does the man whose hopes were fading now with courage look ahead?

Did you leave a trail of kindness, or a scar of discontent?

As you close your eyes in slumber, do you think God will say,
you have earned one more tomorrow by the work you did today?
–John Hall

OO

Do you love God purely?

Any way that men love Me, in that same way they find My love; for many are the paths of men, but they all in the end come to Me.

–Bhagavad Gita XI.23

No man's heart is really dry. You have worldly love for children, family and others. It is the same love, but given to some only. You only have to take it all and give it to God.

How can you develop love for God? You love your CD player. How is it that you have that love? When the CD player was in the shop did you love it? But because you have got it now, it is yours – 'my' CD player is your loving thought for it. You did not love it when it was in the shop; you love it now because you feel "it is mine". So when you think God is "mine", you love Him.

Also, think of the difficult times when God saved you from those ordeals in His miraculous ways, when no earthly help could come to your rescue. Was it not the love of God for you that showered His Grace on you? And if you received such pure love from God time and again, would you not long to return His love in the same manner too?

Remind yourself time and again:

Within the heart
Is enshrined
The Secret of 'Nama'
The Name Divine
The way to unlock the Secret
is the way of love.

Teach me, O Lord,
To love Thee
Not myself
So bless me, that forsaking myself,
I may think of Thy Lotus feet,
By day and by night.

The above was the message of Dada JP Vaswani for the earnest spiritual seeker.

Our attachment should flow towards God like the current of a river. A river *automatically* flows down to the sea. Just as the river is flowing towards the sea, spontaneously, without any artificial attempt, our love should spontaneously flow towards God. That is the perfection of Yoga, which means "union".

Spontaneous love for God does not depend on any external cause. Its only cause is the love itself. Therefore, it is called "causeless love and ceaseless joy", without any motive. Ceaseless joy is something that is unable to be checked. Real love for God cannot be checked by any material condition. If you say: "I am very busy and love to work hard, so I cannot love God. When I get millions of dollars in my bank account, I shall take to God-consciousness", this is not *love* or *bhakti* of God. This is not attachment to Him.

"Your first business of life," says Srila Prabhupada, "is to increase your spontaneous attachment for God. That is the primary business of human life, because only in the human form of life can you do that." By doing so, your life on this planet is successful and you won't have to assume any more material bodies. You will get a spiritual body and go to God – return home to Godhead. Therefore, if you increase your attachment to God, the benefit is that you create a solution for all the problems in your life.

For increasing your attachment to God, in the beginning you have to follow some regulatory principles and restrictions, just as you follow restrictions prescribed by the doctor to cure physical ailments. Similarly, you have to accept certain dos and avoid the don'ts to cultivate godly love favourably. We have to accept *those* things awakening our attachment to God and reject everything else. You cannot argue. That will not help you. We may be addicted to all kinds of wrongdoings, like meat eating, illicit sex, gambling and intoxication, which are the four pillars of sinful life. Unless you stop all such unwanted activities, you cannot attain God-consciousness.

Says Lord Krishna in the *Bhagavad Gita* (6.47): "Of all yogis, one who is always thinking of Me is the best." You can only think of someone if you're attached to him. Otherwise you cannot. It's not possible. If you love somebody, you will always see his picture, his form in your mind. In the same way, the form and fact of the Lord should colour your fantasy and mental world.

In the beginning you have to learn to love God, but when you actually come to the state of love for God, there is no question of "have to". You will then spontaneously follow the regulatory principles because love is present. To express your love, when you offer fruits, flowers, leaves or food items to God, He really accepts them.

Patram pushpam phalam toyam yo
Me bhaktya prayacchatitad aham
Bhakti – upahrtam ashnami
Prayatatmanah.

Lord Krishna says in the *Bhagavad Gita* (9.26): "When My devotee offers Me something within the categories of vegetables, grains, fruits, and water or milk, I accept and eat it because he has brought it with devotion and love."

The devotee thinks: 'God, you have given us so many nice foodstuffs and I have cooked them. Please partake of these preparations first as my grateful thanksgiving to You.' This is love. In fact, you are offering Him back what already belongs to Him and in this way develop your love for Him.

Love Him by chanting His name and by simply hearing about Him. *Shravan, kirtan, sumiran, dhyana*, i.e., hearing, chanting, remembering or contemplation, and meditation are the best ways of getting close to God and learning to love Him.

You will see your life turning a new leaf and your psyche getting transformed gradually. Such is the power of the love of God.

OO

Are you centred outside your Self?

A universal law governs the fact that no one can ever wrong another without being wronged in return: someway, somehow, sometime, somewhere.

–Vikas Malkani

Most of the times our self-centred tendencies and lifestyle force us to think only of our own self or of our immediate family and live only in terms of this narrow circle of our focused attention. When all our activities are self-centred this becomes a great bondage for us. But when we try to do good to others we automatically expand our spiritual horizon and rise above our narrow self. This purifies the heart and increases the *Sattva* in us and removes the *Rajas* and *Tamas* tendencies of our nature. It reduces selfishness and ego, spontaneously bringing abundance and prosperity to us.

Let's consider the example of the colour spectrum. When we perceive a particular colour, say red, it looks red not because it has red colour, but only because it has *not* absorbed the red colour for its own self. The rest of the colours of the prism that have been grabbed and absorbed are not visible in it, and the only colour (red, in this case) that it has surrendered and *not* grabbed is reflected through it. So, in fact, we lose what we grab. In contrast, what we give or offer as service comes bouncing back to us manifold.

As Swami Rama Tirtha maintains: "The expansion of one's self brings about spiritual advancement in life." He calls it "grades of spiritual advancement or degrees in the refinement of selfishness". See the Illustration.

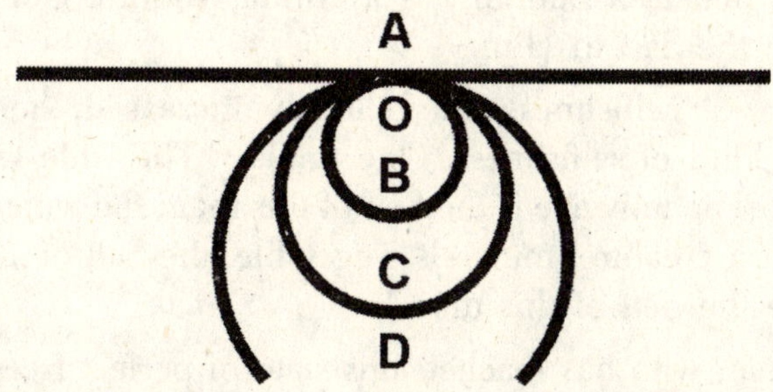

In the above illustration, there is a small circle, then beyond it we have a second circle (B) which is larger than the inner circle, and outside that a third one (C) and then a fourth one (D). One peculiarity of these circles is that as the circles go on expanding and enlarging, the centre of the circle goes on receding from the starting point A, on the straight line, which is a common tangent to all the circles. The centre recedes, the radius increases and the circle enlarges. If the centre of the circle is very near the starting point A and if it is made nearer and nearer, it still coincides with the starting point and the circle becomes a point.

Thus a point is the limiting position of a circle, of which the centre has come extremely near to the starting point, and when the centre goes on receding from the starting point, the radius keeps on increasing until it becomes infinite or the centre moves up to infinity, then the circle becomes a straight line. Thus a straight line is the limiting position of a circle, of which the centre moves up to infinity, or of which the radius is infinite.

The law of nature is that you should not stand still in any position, you should go on – march on and on. In the above illustration, we began with the point of a circle, gross selfishness, and here is that little point enlarged, increased and expanded till it has become a straight line. These are God-men. These are people to whom the wide world is home, irrespective of caste, colour, creed, community or country. Be you an Englishman, an American, a Mohammedan, a Buddhist or a Hindu, you are God's Self. You are the Self to Him.

Here is selfishness marvellously increased; here is a strange kind of selfishness. One thinks, "The wide world is my Self. The universe is the Self of this man; the wide world, the lowest creature, minerals, vegetable, the Self of all these become the Self of this man."

A man who has reached this state of perfect freedom is said to be centred outside his narrow Self. Swami Rama Tirtha quotes another example. To a master of a state of perfect freedom there came a disciple who sat at his feet for a year or so. When the disciple was to leave the master, he began to bow at his feet in order to kneel before him and prostrate himself, as is the custom in India.

Smiling, the master raised him and said: "Dear, you have not yet learnt all that you could learn. You lack a great many things yet; stay for some more time."

He stayed a few more days in the holy presence of the master and received more inspiration. His heart was converted into God-consciousness. He was full of the Divine Spirit. He left the presence of the master, knowing not whether he was the disciple or the master himself. He went away looking upon the whole universe, the wide world, as his real Self, and the whole universe being his real Self, where could he, the Self, go when the Self fills and permeates every atom, every molecule – where can it go? The idea of going and coming becomes meaningless to him. You can go from one place to another if you are not already at the place where you want to go. Here he found himself, he found his true Self, God within, God everywhere, and how could he think of going and coming? He was in a state of Self-realisation. Then the master was satisfied.

Thus did the master test him and prove him to be of sterling worth. Here is the state where one realises: "I am not confined in this body. I am not this little body only – I am the wide world, the boundless Self. I am you and honour me in you." Such a state of mind releases you from all narrow confines of your Self, centring you *outside* your Self.

Are you in such a state of mind? If not, try to attain this.

OO

Are you a Karma Yogi?

To do one's duty is one's right.
But not to hanker for its fruit,
Neither result nor cessation
of action is the Yoga Way.

–Bhagavad Gita II.47

Every morning start your day with thanks to the Almighty for gifting you yet another brand new precious day. And throughout the day, whatever duty you perform should be performed as dedicated to the Lord and for His sake and decidedly not for obtaining their fruits. Treat your work as His work entrusted to you.

"If you are unable to pursue the other practices [such as meditation], be intent to work for Me; you shall attain perfection [in the shape of My realisation] even by performing actions for My sake," says Lord Krishna to Arjuna in the *Bhagavad Gita* (12.10).

The philosophy of Karma Yoga brings man closer to God. We have to also regard our Karma Yoga as a means of pleasing God, of worshipping Him and keeping our ego aside. We must thank God for that opportunity and every other such opportunity. Have humility and the right perspective and approach to Karma Yoga by being aware that we are only an instrument of God and God is the doer, using us as instruments to help His own creatures. He is the father and the mother. He wants to help them all so He is only taking hold of us and through us He helps mankind.

When engaged in Karma Yoga, let us be careful to ensure that in our minds there is no lurking desire for recognition, approval, name or fame. This is a common failure of all aspirants of Karma Yoga. While performing Karma Yoga, one should actually worship the Eternal Divine enshrined in all creatures in the universe. This higher vision and intent makes one's Karma Yoga blemish free.

"The world is imprisoned in its own activity except when actions are performed as worship of God," says the *Bhagavad Gita.* According to the *Gita*, in storing earthly treasures and possessions, there are two provisos one must keep in mind. One is that we must remind ourselves that our worldly possessions are not really ours, but are held in trust for God. Our wealth must be used rightly, and part of it returned to God in the form of help to our fellowmen.

Even our children are not ours. "You can house their bodies, but not their souls," says Kahlil Gibran. Like King Janaka of Aryavartha and Job of the Old Testament, we should mentally and emotionally be unattached to possessions and the position God has given us in this world while still using them with wisdom and humility.

The second proviso is that as one approaches old age, one should detach oneself still further from his treasures on earth and turn his mind wholly to acquiring those spiritual treasures that he *can* take with him through the transition called death. His life must become more oriented away from the material world towards the spiritual. Is it not foolish for a man to spend his last years greedily acquiring worldly wealth, merely for all this to be left behind the moment death makes its inevitable call?

Those who can venture to take this spiritual journey and reorient their values and dedicate their actions and possessions to the Divine power will rise beyond the endless seesaw of life's fleeting joys and pains – the dualities of misery and pleasure of their sensuous indulgence. They shall find perennial peace and happiness, at last.

In the words of Sathya Sai Baba: "Karma is like the trail of dust behind the moving carriage. When the carriage stops, the dust will settle on it. But the carriage cannot forever continue fast along the road in order to escape the dust. The best course is to get on the paved highway, away from the dust-track. That is to say, man must acquire the Grace of God and move along the path smoothened by it."

OO

Are you childlike?

God speaks to us, but we hear Him not.
For we must first regain the child-state,
which we have lost,
before His sound is audible to us.
Blessed are the child-like souls,
for they shall commune with God!

–JP Vaswani

Each one does a particular job in a house, but in the evening, when the family has finished the work and divided the tasks, nobody says: "Father, I did such and such work and you must pay me for that." It is *your own house* and so you just do the work. But when someone from outside comes, you fix the rate and pay accordingly. When you pay them that denotes they are outsiders. But when they become your own, you don't have to pay them. They work with interest and no pay is expected.

Similarly with God, when you think Him to be the nearest and dearest to you, like one family, you don't *ask* for pay. "The one who surrenders like that, he is My own – he does not have to look for payment," says Sathya Sai Baba. But the one who says, "I have done so much *sadhana*" and barters with God, "You give me such and such as a reward", then therein lies the difference. He becomes an outsider by his very asking. The small child does not ask the mother, 'I want milk; I want to be changed' and so on, but the mother looks after every need of the child without its asking.

When you have surrendered yourself completely to God and become God's child, you don't have to tell God what you want. He will give more than you have asked for. But it is only by love that He is your dearest. When you do *sadhana* and feel close to God, you don't have to tell Him that you want this or that. Because you are like a little child, He will come and give you more than what you ask for. His gifts are beyond your asking.

But our ego is what prevents us from getting close to God. The ego makes you think in terms of 'I' – as the doer. You must see "I" as the only instrument of the Lord. Like the fan is an instrument, you are the instrument of the Lord. Do the blades make the fan rotate or is it the current that does so? Obviously the current! The current is God, so you are only the instrument.

Consider God as the ultimate creator and be like a child to receive His full Grace.

OO

Did you knock at the door of God?

I got up early one morning
And rushed right into the day;
I had so much to accomplish
That I didn't have time to pray.
Problems just tumbled about me,
And heavier came each task;
"Why doesn't God help me?"
I wondered.

He answered, "You didn't ask."
I wanted to see joy and beauty,
But the day toiled on grey and bleak,
I wondered why God didn't show me.
He said, "But you didn't seek."
I tried to come into God's presence;
I used all my keys in the lock.
God gently and lovingly chided,
"My child, you didn't knock."

I woke up early this morning,
And paused before entering the day;
I had so much to accomplish
That I had to make time to pray.

–TL Vaswani

OO

Do you know the art of true prayer?

Prayer is a song, a poem, a dance of your heart.

–Osho

There is no experience that can equal the ecstasy of prayer. Prayer is joy. Live in the miracle of prayer. "Don't go to God as a beggar. Prayer is not necessarily asking for something. Prayer is gratefulness; a recognition of the huge tidal waves of love that God is showering on you every moment," says Sri Sri Ravi Shankar.

God is omnipotent, omnipresent and omniscient. You don't have to necessarily go to a temple, a church or a mosque to pray; wherever you pray, God is there. Prayer is not going towards something, which is outside you, Prayer is becoming aware of God within you. It is going deep within.

Prayer is not a mechanical thing, a set routine. It has to rise spontaneously from within. It is not demanding something from God, but having the trust that He knows what is best for you and that whatever is best will happen. Having this confidence in yourself and in God, pray sincerely and earnestly from within the vicissitudes of your heart.

The prayer of the enlightened is the prayer that is full of love – for God, not for one's own desires to be fulfilled. In *japa* and meditation, when you repeat one word again and again, this repetition of sacred words has to be done in a state of total love for God. Before this stage, *japa* has no meaning. Love for God has to be total; the way one recalls and relives moments associated with one's loved one. The heart that yearns for God in prayer and wishes to join the primeval source from where one came (God) knows the art of true prayer.

When you sit in prayer, you have to shed a lot of what might be gross in you. Otherwise your words will ring hollow. You can pray or communicate with God without words but not without faith. "It is better in prayer to have a heart without words than words without a heart," said Mahatma Gandhi.

Prayer is a great sustaining force. It helps us survive crises, tragedies, heartbreaks, sorrows and losses. It keeps hope alive. Psychiatric research reveals that prayer has therapeutic value, especially for mentally and emotionally disturbed persons. People who have faith in God and sincerely say their daily prayers are less prone to emotional disorders as their inner system gets better tuned and fortified to withstand the tensions of present-day living.

Explained Mahatma Gandhi, "Prayer has been my moral and physical salvation in many a trying situation. I have thrown myself in God's hands and from that moment on, a soothing peace flooded my soul and made everything bearable... Only intense prayer has been able to satisfy my hunger for God, and I believe that a soul can never pray enough."

Tennyson was right when he exclaimed, "More things are wrought by prayer than this world dreams of."

OO

Others

Lord help me live from day to day
In such a self-forgetful way,
That ever when I kneel to pray,
My prayer shall be for "Others".

Help me in all the work I do
To ever be sincere and true.
And know that all I do for you
Must needs be done for "Others".

And when my work on earth is done,
And my new work in Heaven's begun
May I forget the crown I've won,
While thinking still of "Others".

"Others", Lord, yes, "Others".
Let this my motto be,
Help me to live for others
That I may live for Thee.

–Anonymous

OO

Do you wish to cross the worldly ocean?

Drawn in and tossed
On the waves of Birth and Death
You sigh and groan in pain, O Man.
Be steady a moment; watch; catch;
within reach
The lifeboat floats.

–Sathya Sai Baba

It is your action of today that will create your destiny tomorrow. "Act consciously," says Vikas Malkani. God's grace is the only means of crossing the worldly ocean of suffering. The Law of *Karma* or the Law of Harvest is directly related to our life. Thus any action we perform and its cause and effect that governs our lives is *Karma.*

The path of *Karma* is rather intricate, to be understood rather simply. Lord Krishna has classified *Karma* under three heads, according to the motive attached to the performance: a) *Karma* – action, b) *Vikarma* – unfair action, and c) *Akarma* – inaction.

Karma is generally said to result in happiness, *Vikarma* in suffering, while *Akarma* is inaction or renunciation of action, which does not produce any reaction. Only activity or inactivity cannot determine the action, forbidden action or inaction. It is the motive alone that makes them what they are. The motive of the doers or renouncers of actions can turn even an action into inaction and vice versa.

The one who fully realises that he is a non-doer, or has dedicated all his actions to God, is not bound by his actions. The key to success is to withdraw your ego of doership. This will transform all mundane activities into liberation or *Moksha*, which is the highest end of *sadhana* – the state when one does not return to this mortal world again.

OO

Is there life beyond death?

The soul dies not, it always is,
No one eternally is damned.
In past, present and future lives
This soul without a tinge of taint.

–Bhagavad Gita II.20

"You and I have passed through many births, I remember them all, whereas you do not," said Lord Krishna to Arjuna in the *Bhagavad Gita*. We experience close ties with our kith and kin but sometimes we come across some person to whom we are drawn irresistibly closer although we may be meeting him for the first time in our life. This is primarily due to the association we have had with him in our past lives. Though physically we might be meeting him for the first time, yet our soul recognises the other soul.

Similarly, the recognition of an *avatar* (incarnation of God) largely depends upon the duration of your association. The longer one's association with God, the more powerful its effect is. His Grace showers upon the one drawn to His divine feet.

"If a blind man cannot see the sun that does not mean the sun is not there or if a man who is interested in climbing ladders cannot see the roses, it is not the fault of the roses," said Osho. To see the sublime and to recognise the divine, you have to be unprejudiced, open and receptive.

Nazar badli to nazaare badle,
Kashti ne badle rukh to kinare badle.

If you alter your perception, the whole scenario changes and if your lifeboat changes its direction, its goals also change, says Bapu Asaram.

Recognise and follow the footsteps of an *avatar.* Do not doubt and despair in mere worldly associations and attachments.

OO

Use the Eight Magic Words to transform your life

When you meet your friend on the roadside or in the marketplace, let the spirit in you move your lips and direct your tongue. Let the voice within your voice speak to the ear of his ear.

For his soul will keep the truth of your heart as the taste of the wine is remembered when the colour is forgotten and the vessel is no more.

–Kahlil Gibran

More than the words we say....
It's the way we reach out.
Day by day with a welcoming hug,
a laugh to share,
a helping hand to show we care....
It's a comforting touch,
a gentle phrase,
an encouraging smile,
a word of praise....
It's a warmth we give right from the start....
Love is the language of the heart.

Words can make or mar your destiny. They are a very powerful medium. As maintained by well-known spiritual leader JP Vaswani, you must learn to use eight magic words in your conversation with others to change your life.

The *first* is *WE.* Most often, we tend to use our much-loved word 'I'. We must abandon our 'I'-centric existence and realise that we cannot do things in life in isolation.

Second, we must always say *Thank You* as and when it is due. These words act like a pep pill for all the efforts someone has put in.

Third, the use of a request *Could You Please,* instead of using an order, would make all the difference to the one with whom you interact. Your request is sure to secure a quick and positive response.

Fourth, try cultivating a desire to lend a helping hand by often asking, *Can I Help You?* The joy of being of some use to others will rebound back to you in great measure.

Fifth, develop the habit of being frank enough to admit a wrong done by you, using the words, *I Admit I Was Wrong.* Many of life's problems and confrontations would be solved if only we could admit our wrongdoings.

Sixth, give praise when it is due with a genuine compliment like *You Have Done a Great Job.* According to Maslow, the behavioural psychologist, recognition and love are the basic needs of a human being, apart from sustenance needs. As it is said, "Man does not live by bread alone." A word of recognition would go a long way in achieving miracles in life's struggle.

Seventh, be grateful and recognise the role others play in your life by making it known to the person in words such as, *"Where Would I Be Without You!"* It is a sure way of getting rid of your own ego and instilling confidence and love in others.

Eighth, in every moment of your existence, you must remember that you are never alone. Everyday repeat to yourself: *"I Am Not Alone, God Is With Me."*

This insight with words can bring about a holistic healing dimension to your relationship with others and your earthly existence.

OO

Your desires and your destiny

Let go of all efforts, search and desires,
for He can be felt only in deep peace and stillness.

–Sri Sri Ravi Shankar

Are you aware that your human body has been secured as a reward for many lives of meritorious activity? That it is valued as a Boat of Divine Grace to cross the raging ocean of this ever changing, ever agitated flow of life?

You are born of desire, live on desire and pass out by desire. Your life, thus, is based on desires or thoughts; so are your actions. You have given birth to your desires and you are bigger than all your desires.

Remember, "Desire for the One leads to the One. Many is a mess," says Sri Sri Ravi Shankar. When you are overcome by your overwhelming worldly desires and get caught up in their whirlpool, your life turns into a mess. Your life, thus, is based on desires or thoughts. As are your desires, so are your actions. As are your actions, so are the fruits thereof. The fruits determine the goal. It follows that your thoughts and desires determine your destiny.

Therefore, see that you cultivate sublime thoughts and desires that lead to righteous lives, realise the highest fruits and strive to reach the supreme goal. Do not settle for the transient, ephemeral and tangible worldly, material desires. Aspire for the invaluable, priceless devotion of the Supreme Creator.... Be like the lotus – holding the head heavenwards and aspiring for it, despite thriving in the muddy pool of water....

Ironically, "Desire kills joy and all desires aim for joy," says Sri Sri Ravi Shankar to the disciples of his Art of Living courses. These pragmatic lines need to be pondered. A whole lifetime is not sufficient to digest this knowledge: *desire kills joy and all desires aim for joy.* Whenever happiness has disappeared from our lives, if we look deeper, we find that it is because of desire. And ironically, all that we desire is happiness! No person, animal or creature desiring unhappiness is ever born.

When our small minds get tired of running here and there, of wandering everywhere after the shadows of material desires, it reaches the conclusion, "My desires have killed my happiness." A person who has conquered his desires can be called the "king of his destiny".

There's an interesting story on desire narrated by Swami Rama Tirtha: There was a nobleman who underwent all the ascetic practices necessary to see the Goddess of Fortune in flesh and blood before him, as he desired wealth. He practised all the mantras, incantations and charms. A million times he repeated chants that were calculated to make him realise the presence of Goddess Lakshmi. Yet She did not appear. Three million times he underwent all the ascetic practices, still the Goddess did not appear. He lost all faith, renounced everything, took up *sannyas*, (asceticism) and became a monk. The very moment he embraced *sannyas*, left his mansion and retired into the forest, he saw the Goddess before him! He cried in disappointment, "Go away! Why are you here now? I want you no more. I am a monk. What has a monk to do with luxury and worldly enjoyment? When I desperately wanted you, you came not; now that I do not desire you, you have come before me."

The Goddess replied calmly, "You yourself stood in the way! So long as you were desirous, you were asserting duality and making a beggar of yourself and that kind of being can acquire nothing. The moment you rise *above* desires and spurn them, you are God, and to God belongs the glory. That is the secret!"

OO

Do you wish to reap the Divine Harvest?

In the words of Swami Sivananada, the way to such a reward is as follows:

- Plant with Truth the seeds of desire for God realisation. Irrigate the mind with the water of purity. Build the fence of right conduct. You will reap the rich harvest of self-realisation.
- Regard the body as the temple of the Lord, Love as the oil and Truth as the cotton wick. Perform worship to the Lord thus.
- Improve your heart. You will see improvement in everything, everywhere.
- Conquest by alms is no conquest; conquer the hearts of others through love and kindness; this is real conquest.
- Cheerfulness is a sign of life, of spiritual growth.
- Every form is a mass of divine condensed energy.
- Energy, success, happiness, abundant health, strength and peace depend upon spiritual practices of pranayama, japa and meditation.
- Listen to a bird. Learn. Take the song and draw joy as a message from God.
- Within the body, there is the heart. Within the heart, there is a little house. This house has the shape of a lotus. Within the energy centre of this lotus dwells the soul (Atman) or Brahman – the Eternal.

- When the senses are controlled, when the heart is purified, all bonds are loosened and freedom is attained. There is constant and increasing remembrance of Atman.
- The entire universe throbs with one Cosmic Life Principle.
- The happiness of all is the great duty of man and the goodness of all is the great duty of his life.

OO

The promise of God

True life is life in God. He has a promise for man and He lives by it sincerely. His promise is for all. Do you wish to be rewarded by it? If so, read on and make it your reality.

- Try and tread on the path that leads towards Me; I shall remove all obstructions on your path.
- Spend a part of your wealth for Me; I shall bestow the treasury of Heavens on you.
- Bear criticism for My sake; I shall shower My Grace upon you.
- Approach Me; I shall nurture and protect you.
- Share My words with others; this shall make you precious.
- Contemplate upon My essential character; I shall grant you the pearl of wisdom.
- Make Me your rescuer; I shall free you from the slavery and bondage of others.
- Shed tears of love for Me; I shall flood your life with the ocean of bliss.
- Become something for My sake; I shall make you invaluable.
- Tread on My path truly; I shall convert you into the Messenger of Peace.
- Surrender totally to Me; I shall bestow fame on you.
- Chant My name; I shall release you from the illusion of the world.
- Be Mine; I shall lay the entire world at your feet.

OO

Do you see the Divine in everything?

He who sees the One Essence
The Lord, pervading all beings,
Immortal, amidst what's mortal life;
The light ablaze in a world that sleeps
As one's own self who sees all things,
And harms not any as one's dear self
With equal love and same concern,
In pleasure, pain, he excels high.
Who knows Me as the All-in-All
And think of Me undividedly,
To them I grant security
And fill them with their wants and needs.

–Bhagavad Gita VIII.27, VI.29,52, IX.22

A dead dog is on the road and crows are pecking at it. People walk by and say, "Oh! What a terrible sight and what horrible smell!" But Jesus was walking by and He said: "What beautiful teeth the dog had, so white and shiny. Nobody brushed them or took care of them but still the dog kept such beautiful teeth." Jesus was showing that one could see the best qualities in even the worst situations. People who are saintly always look at the good and do not get entangled in negativism.

A knife is used both by a surgeon and a villain. The surgeon cuts with his knife to operate upon the patient for his good, but the villain uses the knife to kill and a housewife may use a knife to cut fruit. If all the knives are put in a circle with a magnet at the centre, the magnet will equally attract all the knives. The good or the bad is not in the knives. God is the magnet and all men are attracted to God. Good or bad is not in a human being, but *in the way the mind is used.*

Thus do not fill the mind with thoughts of evil actions that may be perceived in the world. The purpose of all types of divine and spiritual practices is to *train the mind* to see the divine in everything. This you can carry on in everything you do, as your everyday spirituality.

OO

His precious gifts to you

Earth, water, fire, air and ether,
Mind, intellect and ego-sense,
Are eight field forces God creates.
As lower realms His Majesty's
As dream world's pageant real looks.
By mind's revolt in fantasy,
So all this world and creation
Is held cohesive by the Will.

–Bhagavad Gita VII.4, VIII.6

The royal road to the discovery of the gifts of the Supreme Creator lies, as it has from time immemorial, along the pathway of study, concentration, and contemplation to the supreme heights of illumination and liberation.

God plays purposefully. He created the Earth and the Stones – so that we may learn *stability* from them.

Water – so that we may learn flexibility and persistence from it. Water teaches us the power in *softness*, the *victory of yielding.*

Fire – so that we may learn about *warmth* and *light* from it and at the same time recognise its intense ability to *purify* everything it burns.

Air – so that we may learn *acceptance* and *absorption* from it.

Sky – so that we may glimpse the *boundless* in it and understand how to break our own self-imposed limits and instead help us let our spirit soar beyond any such limits.

Lord Krishna explains in the *Bhagavad Gita* that *vayu* (air) comes from Him and that finer than the air is ether. Finer than ether is the mind, finer than the mind is its intelligence, and finer than the intelligence is the soul. But scientists do not know this! They can perceive only gross things. They mention the air, but where does the air come from?

Suppose a rail train is just starting to move. The engine pushes one coach, which pushes another, and so on, until the entire train is moving. And the whole motion originates with the engineer – a living entity. Similarly, in cosmic creation, the Lord gives the first push, and then, by means of many successive pushes, the entire cosmic manifestation comes into being. This is explained in the *Bhagavad Gita* (9.10): *mayadhyaksena prakrtih sûyate sa – caracaram.* "This material nature is working under My direction, O son of Kunti, and is producing all moving and unmoving beings." And a little later:

Sarva-yonisu kaunteya
murtayah sambhavanti yah
tâsâm brahma mahod yonir
aham bija-pradah pita

"All species of life are made possible by birth in material nature, and I am the seed-giving father" (*Bhagavad Gita*, 14.4). For example, if we sow a banyan seed, a huge tree eventually grows and produces millions of new seeds. Each of these seeds, in turn, produces another tree with millions of new seeds, and so on. So the Lord is the original seed-giving father.

Unfortunately, scientists only observe the immediate cause; they do not perceive the remote cause. God is described in the *Vedas* as *Sarva-Karana-Karanam* – the cause of all causes. If you understand the cause of all causes, then you understand everything.

Actually, everything is being maintained by the Sun's energy, but scientists do not know where the Sun's energy comes from. In the *Bhagavad Gita* (15.12) Lord Krishna says:

Yad âditya – gatam tejo
jagad bhâsayates khilam
yac chandramasi câgnau
tat tejo viddhi mâmakam

"The splendour of the sun, which dissipates the darkness of this whole world, comes from Me. And the splendour of the moon and the splendour of fire are also from Me."

Again, Krishna says *Jyotisam ravir amsuman*: Of lights, I am the radiant sun (*Bhagavad Gita*, 10.21). Also, in the eleventh chapter of the *Bhagavad Gita*, Arjuna tells Krishna, *Saúi-sûrya-netram*: "The sun and the moon are among Your great, unlimited eyes."

Although this knowledge is contained in the *Bhagavad Gita*, scientists cannot attain this knowledge by mere speculation. As maintained by Srîla Prabhupâda, man's plight is like the frog in the well. Everyone thinks of things in a relative way, in his own terms. He calls it "frog philosophy". The frog is always thinking of things in relation to his well. He has no power to conceive of the Arabian Sea because the well is his only experience. God is great, but we are thinking of God's greatness in our own terms, in terms of relative greatness.

Some insects are born at night; they grow at night, have their offspring at night, and die at night. They never see the Sun; therefore, they conclude that there is no such thing as day. If you asked this insect about the morning, it would say: "There cannot be any morning." Similarly, even great scholars say that these scriptural statements are all mental speculations.

But only fools can expect the entire cosmic manifestation, which is only matter, to come into being automatically, without a superior energy.

We may have a nice car, but if there is no driver, what is its use? Unless a man knows how to work a machine, unless he pushes a button, the machine does not work.

Similarly, without the superior energy, the material energy cannot act. Behind this wonderful cosmic manifestation is the direction of a superior energy.

Thus God is the centre of everything. If you recognise and remember this in your daily dealings, and thank Him for His unparalleled, unique gifts to you, you would automatically shun any attempts at violence and love His world as His *amaanat* (possession) entrusted to you to be lovingly respected and cared for.

OO

The power of autosuggestion

When a situation around you is bad, think that it could always have been worse. And if the situation is really bad, it can only get better.

–Vikas Malkani

Psychological research reveals that our mind controls our body. With the power of positive thoughts, you can take charge of your body to maintain perfect fitness, health, strength and happiness. When you repeat a positive thought about yourself, you feed it to your subconscious mind in the way you feed data in the computer. Each person has the capability of programming his own mind to achieve what he desires.

You too can tap this capability by following some simple steps of autosuggestion:

Step I

Be completely relaxed and in a conscious, willing state of mind.

Step II

Make affirmative suggestions such as (or ones modified as per your wish):

- "I can easily get up early in the morning to meditate upon God."

Or

- "I attune myself with Nature and the Divine Force, to stay healthy, confident, and fit to proceed on my spiritual journey."

Or

- ❖ "I can relax into sound sleep and wake up revitalised, alert, bright and cheerful to receive the new day as a precious gift from God."

You can also dissolve most of your mental problems by affirming:

- ❖ "I can dissolve all my health problems, worries and fears easily, quickly and successfully in simple, easy and positive ways by the grace of God."

In this way, you can heal all your psychosomatic sicknesses to a great extent by mentally repeating to yourself, "Day by day, in every way, I'm getting better and better."

Your subconscious mind has the knowledge, power, wisdom and understanding to heal and maintain perfect mental and physical health. Use affirmations to charge your subconscious mind with their healing vibrations, and divine healing prayers.

Say to yourself as you go to bed each night: "Attuned with universal healing powers and the source of all life, all my body organs are now becoming normal and fit, and they will function perfectly to maintain my vital life energy in excellent health, strength and vitality for my body, mind, and spirit."

The following lines unfold the immense power of autosuggestion:

If you think you are beaten, you are.
If you think you dare not, you don't.
If you like to win, but you think you can't,
It is almost certain you won't.
If you think you'll lose, you're lost.
For out of the world we find,
Success begins with a fellow's will,
It's all in the state of mind.
If you think you are outclassed, you are.

You've got to think high to rise,
You've got to be sure of yourself before
You can ever win a prize.
Life's battles don't always go,
To the stronger or faster man,
But sooner or later the man who wins
Is the man WHO THINKS HE CAN!

One.... Two.... Three.... Four....

Keep counting your success throughout life.

❍❍

Do you trust yourself?

For today, if you keep God by your side, there is nothing that will come into your life that you won't be able to handle.
–Vikas Malkani

The quality of your life and your trust in yourself depends on how you are within yourself. Unless you do something to the inner self, you will not know how to go beyond the limitations of being just a body and mind.

Your body may be sick and your physical heart may not function properly, yet within your soul – the spiritual heart – dwells the Spirit of God who ever healeth and blesseth. Each day the Spirit is renewing your body, mind, and heart. And you feel strong, radiant and serenely happy. Each one of you is a storehouse of infinite strength because you are directly connected to the source of infinite power. You are not a candle to be lit by somebody else, but the self-effulgent sun. You have to tap into this inner reserve of endless power instead of relying on an external source.

Remember that your stay in this world is not permanent. You are here only for a picnic. One who goes for a picnic returns home. In the same way, this world is like a transit stop en route to our real home, which is God, our true self.

You are a child of the universe,
No less than the trees and the stars....
You have a right to be here
And therefore be at peace with yourself.

–St Paul

OO

Love – the nectar of life

More than anything else, our greatest lack is love and appreciation. The only way to receive love is to give it. So give it in abundance. Don't ration it!
–Vikas Malkani

Just as the whole universe is governed by principles, in like manner, spirituality too is governed by principles. Spirituality is a way of life – an attitude of life.

Science says that the entire universe comprises energy; spirituality says that the essence of the universe is love. Love = Energy. When we have access to this love, then the whole universe cooperates with us. When that love is flowing within us, we must experience and give this love.

"Love is the deep desire to bless Existence," says Sri Sri Ravi Shankar. When we practise such an attitude, all the resources of the universe would be available to us.

Remember to stop being unkind to yourself. First and foremost you must learn to love yourself. What does this mean? Accept yourself as you are and take care of your self-esteem, becoming aware of your Self and aligning your Self with the Almighty. Know that loving yourself means being an individual and being indivisible, i.e., not labelling, judging or condemning yourself. Otherwise you will always find a *gap* between "what is" and what "should be". So accept "what is" and be truthful to yourself.

When you love yourself, the same love starts flowing towards others in the universe. In love, the unreal dies. Only the heart can speak or hear that which is authentic. Empathy is vital for love. Feel the pain of others. “Pain is a very essential experience in life. You will never experience love otherwise, as love also brings pain,” says Sri Sri Ravi Shankar.

“Every time you feel pain in your heart or in your mind, you can turn it into an experience of great love,” he adds. He talks about the laws of love as:

- The *first law* of love is in understanding that in general the same hopes, sorrows, joys, troubles, and fears encompass us all. The same Destiny beckons us. The same Love enfolds us. The same Justice educates us. The same spark of the Divine permeates us.
- The *second law* of love is that each living creature – superhuman, human, subhuman – through his own individual circumstances of personality in terms of physical, emotional, mental and higher consciousness, and in terms of nationality, faith, race, and environment, is unfolding his being to perfection. Whatever differences there may be, they do not normally imply superiority and inferiority. Love and justice rule the world and are their birthright too.
- The *third law* of love is that we would grow a great deal more swiftly if we could only understand the role of love in life. If we could look back and see that we have grown in understanding, patience, sympathy, and tolerance, then surely we have not lived in vain; for these are the "treasures in heaven" which we can take away with us through the gateway of death and bring back again with us through the gateway of the next birth.

For him who has perception, a mere sign is enough. For him who does not really heed, a thousand explanations are not enough.

Love every act of the Lord – every event of his Great Plan. You will understand something of the wonders and mysteries of the universe when you know that things which seem evil from the side of form are good from the side of life; all that happens is working for the best. Such an understanding can come to us when we have complete trust in God, as trust means love. You cannot love without trust.

In the words of Kahlil Gibran: "Love has no other desire but to fulfil itself. But if you love and must have desires, let these be your desires:

To melt and be like a running brook that sings its
melody to the night.
To know the pain of too much tenderness.
To be wounded by your own understanding of love;
And to bleed willingly and joyfully.
To wake at dawn with a winged heart and give
thanks for another day of loving;
To rest at noon hour and meditate love's ecstasy;
To return home at even tide for the beloved in your heart
And a song of praise upon your lips."

OO

Giving

Who hates no creature, friend of all,
Compassionate to men and things,
Ego-less, mine-less, mind composed,
Forbearing, content, steadfast, poised,
Homeless and rooted in one's aim,
That blessed one hails excellent,
On earth as also in heaven,
Is loved by God as best of men.
–Bhagavad Gita VII.13,19

Give while you can or soon there will come a day when you will be unable to give even if you wish to. The shady tree does not wait for a proper time or choose a special person to nurture with its cool shade. It makes no distinction of time, caste, creed or religion for giving its service. Give like the tree – spontaneously, unconditionally and selflessly – without the desire of a favour in return. Be helpful to as many as you can. Consider no one as unworthy of your love and give the service of your help to all. God helps him who serves selflessly.

In the words of Kahlil Gibran: "You give but little when you give of your possessions. It is when you give of yourself that you truly give. For what are your possessions but things you keep and guard for fear you may need them tomorrow? And what is fear of need but need itself? Is not dread of thirst when your well is full the thirst that is unquenchable?"

The hidden desire for recognition makes one's giving totally unwholesome. When you give, give gladly without knowing pain or seeking joy, or with mindfulness of virtue. Give as the blooming flower breathing its fragrance into space.

"Through the hands of such as these God speaks, and from behind their eyes He smiles upon the earth," adds Gibran.

It is well to give when asked, but better still to give unasked, through understanding. See first that you yourself deserve to be a giver and an instrument of giving. For in truth, it is life that gives unto life while you, who deem yourself a giver, are a witness.

And as receivers, assume no weight of gratitude, lest you lay a yoke upon yourself and upon him who gives. "Rather rise together with the giver on his gifts as wings; for to be over-mindful of your debt is to doubt his generosity who has the freehearted earth for mother, and God for father," Gibran says.

And how should one give one's offering to God? Says Lord Krishna in the *Bhagavad Gita* (IX.26): "If one offers Me with love and devotion a leaf, a flower, fruit or water, I will accept it." He is just like the loving father who accepts even the most insignificant gift of his little child purchased with his (father's) own money. The significance of his gift lies not in the cost of the gift but in the *attitude* of love behind the giving.

Thus, when we begin to learn to give with the attitude of love and without a latent desire of receiving something in return, the giving becomes genuine and pure. So give genuinely and innocently like a child.

OO

Are you aware of your focus in life?

He that offers God a second place, offers Him no place.
–Bapu Asaram

Unaware of the real focus in our life, most of us wander in the labyrinths of life, drifting by like a paper boat in the midst of an ocean. "A wise man knows not only what to look at but also what to overlook," contends Vikas Malkani.

In the words of Dada JP Vaswani, our focussing in life should be in the following pattern:

"O mind!
why dost thou wander from object to object?
Whatever has happened had to happen.
Knowing this, do not worry over the past,
nor be concerned about the future.
Cling to the lotus feet of the Lord
and there find true beauty, joy and peace!"

He also expresses focusing on God in these simple and thoughtful verses:

"So many are eager to fly into outer space,
to reach the moon,
to dwell on Mars!
My soul yearns to enter within,
where Thou dost dwell,
the Self of my self."

As long as you focus on the world and its material activities, your chattering mind gets full of the illusionary world and its attractions. Thus you fail to get the attention of God. Just as when you dream, all the activities you perform during the dream look very real to you, but the moment you are awakened from your sleep, you realise it was all unreal. Similarly, when you are in this world, you feel that your focus should be on worldly activities only, which is akin to your illusion in the dream state.

Unless we are spiritually awakened, we cannot realise that we are focusing our energies in vain on illusionary activities. To reach the innermost chamber of our heart, where our soul dwells, we have to cross many sheaths covering our soul. Only if we take away our mind from material longings can we attain the attention of God or God realisation to reach the ultimate goal of human life.

He who is fully occupied in his desire for God has no time in this world to consider who is friend or foe, kin or stranger. The offering up, the consecration of physical, emotional, mental, or any other energy, at the Divine Altar – this indeed is truly described as the whole of Bhakti Yoga.

"He is the sole owner of the cosmos, silently showering man with gifts from life to life. There is but one gift man may offer in return – his love, which he is empowered to withhold or bestow," says Swami Paramahansa Yogananda.

If you remind yourself of your original nature – your original source – you would experience a nostalgic bond with Almighty God, as expressed in the words of Adi Guru Shankaracharya:

"Mind, nor intellect, nor ego, feeling;
Sky nor earth nor metals am I.
I am He, I am He, Blessed Spirit,
I am He!

No birth, no death, no caste have I;
Father, mother, have I none.

I am He, I am He, Blessed Spirit,
I am He!

Beyond the flights of fancy, formless am I,
Permeating the limbs of all life;
Bondage I do not fear; I am free, ever free,
I am He, I am He, Blessed Spirit,
I am He!"

Shankaracharya further clarifies his views thus: "A true yogi may remain dutifully in the world; there he is like butter on water, and not like the non-churned, easily diluted milk of undisciplined humanity. Fulfilling one's earthly responsibilities need not separate man from God, provided he maintains mental non-involvement with egotistical desires and plays his part in life as a willing instrument of the Divine."

Meditation and the Self within

With the mind not moving towards any other thing,
made steadfast by the method of habitual meditation,
and constantly meditating, one goes to the Supreme Person,
the Resplendent, O Arjuna.
Thus by practice incessant and firm,
allowing not the mind to roam,
in divine love's saturation,
The Supreme Person is attained.
–Bhagavad Gita VIII.9,10

"At the time of death, unshaken mind endowed with devotion, by the power of Yoga, fixing the whole life-breath in the middle of the eyebrows, he reaches that resplendent Supreme Person," adds Lord Krishna and elucidates, "I am easily attainable by that ever steadfast Yogi who constantly and daily remembers Me (for a long time) not thinking of anything else, (with one-pointed mind), O Arjuna."

Meditation for most of us is a silent and calming process. Guided meditation makes you look deeply within, into your self, face your suffering and be free of its bondage. In fact, it has been in practice since the time of Buddha. References to meditation can be found in the Sutra for the sick and dying. Research reveals that meditation developed in India around 2750–1500 BC.

The word *meditation* is derived from two Latin words *meditari* (*to think about, contemplate*) and *medri* (*to heal*). At its root lies the concept that meditation is not just an enlightening exercise, but is also equally essential for a healthy mind and body.

In his book *Meditation and Life*, Swami Chinmayananda contends, "Meditation has been glorified as the most sacred vocation. Humans alone are capable of this highest effort by which they can hasten their own evolution."

As the ability to look within is a prerequisite to meditation, you have to learn by practice to be a silent observer of your inner life and estimate your motives, intentions and purposes that lie behind your thoughts, words and deeds. The idea of this self-analysis is to accept your psychological make-up as it is – with its glories as well as inadequacies.

"Your first analysis," explains Swami Chinmayananda, "may seem like the narration of the ideal life lived by gods." This is so because most of us perceive ourselves this way most of the times. As though we can do no wrong! And even if we do wrong, it is for a larger good! Which is why the analysis should try and detect the dark nature, the shadow self that lies hidden under layers and layers of justifications.

But without sufficient preparation, this can also cause psychological disorders such as paranoia and depression. Which is why there are many techniques prescribed to achieve the correct state of mind, including prayer, relaxation routines, pranayama, sitting in silence, practising general self-enquiry and chanting mantras.

This stage, according to most meditators, is only the beginning. This is 'catharsis', the process of cleaning your system of its clogging miasma and preparing you for a glimpse into your untouched soul. It is only when the mind is free of its past baggage that the journey within can begin.

"Meditation," wrote Swami Rama, founder of the Himalayan Institute of Meditation, "is a specific technique for resting the mind and attaining a state of consciousness that is totally different from the normal waking state." Because, in meditation, "You are fully awake and alert, but your mind is not focused on the external world or the events taking place around you. Neither is your mind asleep, dreaming or fantasising. Instead, it is clear, relaxed and inwardly focused."

When you meditate you try to draw your concentration inwards and withdraw it from outside forces. In doing so, your mind attains peace, is calm and focussed within. When the mind is calm and still, it slows down considerably in its brainwave frequencies (approximately 4–8 cycles per second). There are four levels of brain activity – beta, alpha, theta and delta.

Generally, the majority of us use more of the left-brain hemisphere and are beta-dominated. When you meditate you go more into alpha and theta. The two brain hemispheres, right and left, begin to communicate effectively. Alpha patterns are associated with calm and focused attention, theta with reverie and creativity. In contrast, when your mind is actively involved in external activities, it takes 20–25 brainwave cycles per second. The slowing of brainwaves also slows down your blood pressure, and the pulse rate, giving your body and mind rest and rejuvenation. This, in turn, causes better concentration and efficiency of the mind and better physical health. In this way, one works more efficiently in one's work sphere.

For this reason, more and more organisations are today propagating meditation and allowing an exclusive meditation period to their employees, even during their working hours during the day. This equips them to work better with more concentration and efficiency.

The research findings of doctors today reveal that people who meditate have fewer illnesses in contrast to those who do not. Their immune system is fortified and their endurance mechanism improves. As a result, it reduces absenteeism in offices and turnover is enhanced.

While you meditate inwards and feel an inexplicable peace within your self, for the first time you begin to really believe that there is an element of God within your self. This new belief and realisation inspires you with a new awareness that just as you feel the presence of God within you, likewise other human beings, animals, birds and even inanimate things possess the same element of God within them. This stark realisation fills you with empathy and kindles in you the desire to help and nurture them.

Thus, you become loving and helpful towards the *entire universe* and not just your own family. Just as you psychologically free yourself from the bondage of the confines of your ego and your limited selfish ends, your spiritual entity widens. It becomes larger than life, enabling you to attain the main mission of your human existence – maximum good to maximum humanity.

Dr Andrew Newberg of the University of Pennsylvania, USA, studied the effects of meditation on Tibetan monks through brain-imaging techniques. On comparing the brain activity of people performing Tibetan Buddhist meditation with what their brains did at rest, it was revealed that meditation increased activity in the front part of the brain and decreased activity in the area of the brain that orients our bodies in space. Thus, the change in spatial perception takes place and the loss of the subjective identification of the self during meditation. In this connection, the modern meditator's technological breakthrough in finding a shortcut to the meditative state through mind machines and artificial stimulation of certain parts of the brain are classic examples of our machine age!

Today, meditation has been accepted as one of the most effective remedies for stress and stress-related disorders such as high blood pressure, insomnia, and heart diseases. It enhances the immune system. Research has revealed that nursing home residents trained in meditation have increased activity of natural-killer cells that kill bacteria and cancer cells. They also have reduced activity of viruses and emotional distress.

But accepting meditation as part of a healthy lifestyle would be grossly underrating a technique that is often believed to be the key to self-realisation. In essence, meditation is not a technique to be practised, but "a way of life".

"Meditation," explains Swami Krishnananda of the Divine Life Society, "is the art of uniting with Reality." As long as we treat it as a chore or a disciplinary measure, its truth will elude us.

"The purpose of meditation is to awaken the sky-like nature of the mind, and introduce that which we really are –our unchanging pure awareness. While meditating, neither follow thoughts nor invite them; be like the ocean looking at its own waves, or the sky gazing down on the clouds that pass through it," says Sogyal Rinpoche in his book, *The Tibetan Book of Living and Dying.*

For J Krishnamurti, meditation does not mean religious or scriptural practices, but reaching within one's 'self' and opening up to the universe all around. He says: "Meditation implies awareness, awareness of the earth, the beauty of the earth, the dead leaf, the dying daylight, to be aware of the beauty of the wind among the leaves, to be aware of your thoughts, your feelings. That means to be aware without choice – just to be aware....

"And when you are so aware, then there is attention. When you so profoundly attend, there is no centre as the 'me' to attend.

"And when there is attention, there is silence.... That silence has never been touched by thoughts. It is only the mind that is utterly free from all the travails of life, it is only such a mind that can find the Supreme."

Consider the poem on the opposite page. Does it hold true for you?

Do you ever meditate?

You fix up the time, regular and punctual
And you plan to meditate.
You take a bath, become clean and fresh
And you get ready to meditate.
You select a corner, dark and cool
And you desire to meditate.
You prepare the seat, soft and clean
And you wish to meditate.
You bring the flowers, fresh and fragrant
And you decide to meditate.
You burn incense and rich perfumes
And you aspire to meditate.
You sit in asana, straight and still,
And you try to meditate.
You chant, breathe and concentrate,
And you think you meditate.
And with all these preparations and plans of mind,
Do you ever become free from thought to meditate?
Do you ever meditate?

When you meditate do you feel:

- Your stress levels are reduced drastically?
- Your personal effectiveness increases?
- Your quality and productivity levels at work are improved?
- Your body becomes very light or very heavy during meditation?
- Your body feels very cold or it perspires?
- You can hear clearly the beating of your heart from inside during meditation?
- Feel the hot gases going out of your ears?
- Your body goes into various yogic postures/ movements?
- You experience sudden laughter or crying?

- Your body sways front to back or sideways or whirling sensations are felt even when the physical body is steady. (This is because of the astral body trying to separate from the physical.)
- You feel that something has gone out of your body and feel afraid of it? (Fear is common and there is no need to specially worry about such fears. A better way to handle fear is to face it squarely as and when it arises. By doing so it will rise to its peak and then subside.)
- You feel sleepy. (It is not 'sleep' though – a thought-free state of mind gives such a feeling initially.)

If so, you are on the right track. Keep it up!

OO

Do you have faith in God?

Faith is the bird that ***feels*** *the light*
and sings when the dawn is still dark.
–Rabindranath Tagore

"If you are based in faith," says Sri Sri Ravi Shankar, "you move with all possibilities. If you are based in mind and intellect with all their limitations, you will become inert." The grace of the Supreme Creator has to be *felt* with your heart, and not calculated with your mind.

A subtle couplet expresses a similar thought thus:

The best and the most beautiful things in this world
Cannot be seen or even touched
They must be felt with the heart.

God is always close to us regardless of our circumstances. It is we who are far away from Him. His love is boundless, unconditional and unlimited. In return, He asks for our sincerity alone. If we need genuine help, all we have to do is to ask, and often not even that. He gives us more, even beyond our asking.

The verses below reflect His generosity beautifully:

More than hearts can imagine
or minds comprehend
God's beautiful gifts
are ours without end.
We ask for a cupful
When the vast sea is ours.

We pick a small rosebud
from a garden of flowers.
Whatever we ask for
falls short of God's giving.
For His greatness exceeds
every facet of living.

The farmer sows seeds with faith in existence, losing the seeds he holds in his hand and gaining much more. When you know, you have faith, when you don't know, then you start believing. In the words of Sathya Sai Baba: "Faith is that state of being beyond both certainty and doubt, unaffected by the alternation of opposites; it is the point of equilibrium wherein all sufferings cease."

Do you think God would confront you with pain where there is no reason for it? Open your heart to pain, as you do for pleasure, for it is His will, wrought by Him for your good. Welcome it as a challenge. Do not turn away from it. Turn within and derive the strength to bear it and benefit by it. Unpleasant experiences come and go. Accept them with the power of the Self. Tell yourself, "If what I want for myself is contrary to what God wants for me, let me want only what God wants, and I shall be at peace."

Often God speaks to us but we hear Him not! For we must first regain the child-state that we have lost, before His sound is audible to us. Blessed are the childlike souls, for they shall commune with God.

As a saying goes: "Faith has everything; cynicism has none." In the words of the great master Osho: "To see the sublime, to see the divine, you have to be unprejudiced; you have to be open and receptive.... It is like the sun rising in the morning; the sun cannot give life to a flower – no! But the flower opens itself towards it and is enriched through its own opening."

You can even converse with God and listen to Him. God speaks to us through our inner voice – our conscience, our inner self. We can commune with Him through the inner recesses of our heart. Our unwavering and unflinching faith in Him even during our dark times makes us whole.

Know that God gives you a chance to work out your *karma* through times of adversity. Problems on the job, challenges, betrayals and illnesses are the acid tests of our Spiritual Intelligence Quotient. Have a willingness to embrace anything that may happen.

Says philosopher Echart Tolle: "Surrender is the simple but profound wisdom of yielding to rather than opposing the flow of life. To surrender is to accept the present moment unconditionally and without reservation. It is to relinquish inner resistance to what is."

So speak each word, perform each action, face each situation before an inner altar where you kneel in utmost adoration and self-surrender, under the seal and sign of your highest Self.

OO

Footprints

For all that God in his mercy sends,
For health and children, home and friends;
For comfort in the time of need,
For every kindly word and deed;
For happy thoughts and holy talk,
For guidance in our daily walk –
For everything give THANKS!
–Anonymous

One night a man had a dream. He dreamed he was walking along the beach with the Lord. Across the sky flashed scenes from his life. For each scene, he noticed two sets of footprints in the sand – one belonging to him and the other to the Lord. When the last scene of his life flashed before him, he looked back at the footprints in the sand. He noticed that many times along the path of his life, there was only one set of footprints. He also noticed that it happened at the lowest and saddest times of his life.

This really bothered him and he questioned the Lord about it: "Lord, You said that once I decided to follow You, You would walk with me all the way. But I have noticed that during the most troublesome times in my life, there is only one set of footprints. I don't understand why when I needed You most, You would leave me."

The Lord replied: "My son, My precious child, I love you and would never leave you. During your times of trial and suffering, when you saw only one set of footprints, it was then that I carried you."

Seek God when still young

I do not seek pleasure! Pleasure makes a man sick!
I do not seek possessions: possessions possess the possessor!
I do not seek power: power makes a man corrupt!
I do but yearn for thee, O Lord!
So bless me, that everyday of my life may rise as an offering unto Thee! Mayst Thou be my Unseen Companion in all my ways of living!
–JP Vaswani

Most of us have the tendency to think of God as secondary to our life's endless routine. Our thought-pattern often runs like this: "I have so many responsibilities to fulfil – where is the time for prayer? After my retirement, when I am free, I shall then take to meditation and worship of God." Isn't that ridiculously illogical?

In this context, Sri Asaram often narrates an interesting and meaningful anecdote. There was a woman serving her mother-in-law late at night. She looked fatigued after her routine household chores. Observing her sleepy eyes, the mother-in-law asked her to retire to bed and take rest, if she was through with all her chores. The woman affirmed that she had finished *all* the household work.

The next morning, when the daughter-in-law began her day, the mother-in-law asked her the same question: "Are you free? You had finished all the work last night."

The daughter-in-law retorted apprehensively: "Oh no! All the morning chores have to be done – cooking and packing the children's tiffin, bathing and cleaning them and all the washing and cooking for the day."

Here lies the crux of the matter! Though she thought she had finished *all* her routine chores the night before, it was awaiting her afresh the very next morning.

Well! How can you ever think that there will be days when you shall be free from your mundane activities of the day to devote yourself to the worship of God? After wasting the prime of your youth – the best years of your life – in worldly pursuits, would you wish to offer God the years of your old age when your body and mind have already deteriorated and weakened with old age, disease and the invariable disillusionment of life? Is that the quality of time you would like to offer His name, He who has bestowed on you the most precious gift – your very life? Isn't that tragic?

Indeed, when we give God a secondary position, we give Him no position at all. Don't you find time to take your meals everyday? In like manner, make it a way of life to meditate upon the name of God everyday right from the early years of your life. It will enlighten your destiny and your entire persona.

Most of us hardly realise that time is most precious, as it never returns. All the time it flies past without our awareness. You are growing old everyday. When the clock rings, you hear one hour being cut off from your lifespan. In fact, the moment you are born, death exists side by side with birth. Cells grow and decay. Human birth is attained with great difficulty, after 8.4 million animate and inanimate incarnations.

Human birth is the only golden opportunity for God realisation, as this is not possible in *any* other incarnation. The human form is the only form through which God can be realised. Who knows how many years one has to live during one's lifetime? How do you know whether you will ever reach your "retirement" or "old age"? It is said, "Man proposes, God disposes." So how can you take your lifetime for granted?

Then why not worship God right through the spring of your human life? Become a successful person in your life and become a devotee, right from this very moment. Remind yourself that everyday death is drawing near. So time cannot be wasted in earning one's living and enjoying worldly pleasures alone. Else, when shall you realise the real goal of your life – God realisation? When shall you free yourself from the wheel of births and deaths?

Haven't you heard the story of a man who wanted his thirsty horse to quench its thirst by drinking water? He took the horse to a nearby *rahat* (a machine for drawing water). As the machine made a noise when it drew water through its wheels, the horse refrained from drinking the water. But when the noise stopped, the water also stopped. Hence it became impossible for the horse to drink the water. The *rahat* owner then advised the perplexed owner of the horse that if his horse was really interested in quenching its thirst, he had no option but to train it to drink from the noisy machine. Your plight is exactly like that of the thirsty horse. The noise from mundane activities of your worldly life is never going to cease. So you have to train yourself to remember God's name and worship Him amidst life's routine, its noise and its hustle and bustle.

Half your life is spent in sleep. A great portion goes in sickness. Some portion is spent in eating, drinking and talking. In your childhood, you are enveloped in your innocence and spend it in play. Youth catches you in its emotional trap of attraction for the opposite sex. In middle age, you are pressurised by psychological stress and anxieties of your career and family. Old age, as you know, is most demanding and threatening with inevitable health hazards. When will you, my dear friend, find time to do virtuous deeds and contemplation on God?

Says Swami Sivananda, the founder of Divine Life Society and author of over 300 spiritual books: "A doctor speaks on the telephone and ascends the staircase to have his breakfast and is found dead on the staircase itself, on account of a cardiac failure. A princess drives a car along with her husband and loses her life on the way in an accident. Such is the uncertainty and evanescence of life, and yet man foolishly wastes his time."

Just as worldly people engaged in business are very careful about their time, since time is money for them, so also spiritual aspirants are careful about their time and they use it in contemplation upon God. They will not waste their time in idle gossip. They aspire to spend every moment in the service of God. That is the reason they observe *mauna* (remain silent for a fixed period of time). If you take care of the moments, the hours will take care of themselves. Realise God. Shut yourself in a room. Reflect. Meditate. Unfold the hidden spiritual consciousness.

You will have realised the ultimate aim of your precious life and your mind will be filled with *Sattva* (purity). You will gradually develop balance of mind, inner spiritual strength and a strong will. You will feel an inner urge to lead a spiritual life. Seek the company of the spiritually enlightened – saints and mahatmas – and study spiritual scriptures like the *Bhagavad Gita*, the *Upanishads*, the *Ramayana*. This is known as *Satsang* and *Svadhyaya* – company of the enlightened. Attend religious workshops, spiritual discourses and meditation groups.

Today, men find no time to study philosophical and religious books. You can listen to devotional music albums and watch devotional channels on television as you start your day in the wee hours of the morning and also before going to bed. The company of spiritual masters through their life-enhancing discourses over TV channels is a great boon for modern man.

"Companionship of the great ones is again difficult of attainment. It is hardly possible to assign how and when men may be taken into the society of the great. But once obtained, association with the great ones is infallible in its operation...." (*Narad Bhakti Sutras: 39*).

Again, "Companionship of the great ones is gained by the touch of divine compassion and the grace of God alone...." (*Narad Bhakti Sutras: 40*). This is because there is no distinction between Him and His men.

OO

Are you compassionate and unattached?

There are two ways that one can spread light in this world – either by becoming a candle or by becoming a mirror that reflects.
–Vikas Malkani

Compassion stems from wisdom. It is the fundamental law of Nature's own heart. It allows one to become one with the Divine Universe, with the universal life and consciousness. Compassion denotes harmony, peace, bliss, and impersonal love.

It automatically brings happiness and calmness. We reach a point in life when we are satiated with ourselves and life demands that we turn outward towards other human life; when we cease being the passive vessel and ourselves become the living spring.

When we are bound to another human being in triumph and disaster, we are lifted above the passions of pity and envy; his grief is our grief; his joy is our joy; we are one in a union of hearts.

Hatred, jealousy and excessive attachment cause suffering and agitation. Compassion helps you overcome these to move into a calm state of mind. Peace of mind is vital for good health. Experiments show that it is easier for those who practise love and compassion to regain a peaceful state of mind after being agitated. Practise of compassion actually calms you down considerably and builds up your emotional intelligence.

Compassion based on expectation is not true compassion but attachment. Real compassion is doing good to all and sundry without expectations – not just one's friend or known persons. A bee that has made honey does not call out for others to come and see. Likewise a compassionate man who has done a good act does not draw the attention of others, but simply goes on to another compassionate act, as a vine goes on producing grapes again in season.

From the myriad men and women whose great gift is love of wife, or husband, child or parent or friend, the plan of God asks for deeds of tenderness and bravery, those seemingly trivial incidents of a smile and a touch of the hand that encourage another to go on his way unflinchingly towards his goal.

Lord Buddha was once asked why a man should love all persons equally. "Because," the great teacher replied, "in the numerous and varied life-spans of each man, every other being (at one time or another, and in one form or another – animal or human) has been dear to Him."

Remember that it is of the Lord's mercies that we are not consumed, because His compassion fails not. They are new every morning. Human beings become human beings only when they have learned to *feel* for others, for this is the meaning of compassion. It is the crown of consciousness marking the king among men. Such a crown does not signify conquest or power over others, but conquest and power over the self, besides which there is no other real power or glory.

The degree to which you are sensitive to other people's suffering is the index of your own empathy and humanity. It is the root not only of social living but also to the adherence of human consideration. Help your needy brother and you shall be helped yourself, thanks to the never failing and ever active Law of Compensation.

A kindly thought sent out towards some other human being is a protection to the other and it is a beautiful thing to do. It is truly humane and one that every sensitive human being loves to do. Do not judge rashly or interpret the actions of others in an ill sense, but be compassionate to their infirmities, bear their burdens, excuse their weaknesses and make up for their defects – this is the true spirit of compassion and charity.

Compassion is in realising that the other person is also just like you. This recognition is the basis on which you can develop compassion, not only towards those around you but also towards your enemy. Treat your enemy also as a human being. Genuine compassion should be unbiased and flow towards all sentient beings, irrespective of friends or foes.

The term 'Universal Brotherhood' is not an idle phrase.... it is the only secure foundation for universal morality. If it be a dream, it is at least a noble one for mankind. We must aim only at striving to channel better the love power of the universe, that we may add to the sum total of happiness in this world and try to lift a little of the collective *karma* of the world.

When we have reached the sublime goal, we shall have the impulse to turn around, as do the glorious Buddhas of compassion, who turn backward on the path and help our fellows trailing behind. This compassionate act is what true spiritual saviours of men do.

OO

Acceptance

Self-controlled, firm in conviction,
With mind and reason fixed on God,
From whom the world shrinks not in hate,
Who shrinks not from the world around.
Free ever from both joy and grief,
Depending not on things mundane,
Ev'r pure and prompt and unconcerned
Untroubled in his being's core.
–Bhagavad Gita XII.14,15

When it flies high, a bird just glides. You have to glide or float along in life with full acceptance of the Lord – a childlike trust. And to trust God is to accept His Will in *all* conditions and circumstances of life. It entails rejoicing in all that happens. In sickness and suffering, in loss of possessions and power, in danger, disaster and death, let the heart sing: "Irrespective of my thinking, belief, desire or conviction, O Lord, Thy Will be done."

OO

Do you possess a balanced mind?

To those devotees who constantly love Me,
think of Me, worship Me and
remain ever united in thought with Me,
I bring full security and personally
attend to their needs in this world and the next.
–Bhagavad Gita IX.22

Most of us possess three kinds of temperament and three kinds of minds: (i) of unstable equilibrium, (ii) of stable equilibrium and (iii) of neutral equilibrium. Let us look at each kind with the help of a small exercise. Place a pencil vertically upon your palm. You will see that it never balances. For a second or so it may be at rest but every whiff of wind will topple it. This is called *unstable equilibrium.*

If you hold the pencil by one end (i.e. hold it between your fingers and keep it hanging like a pendulum) it is at rest, but being a *pendulum, it will keep oscillating* for some time, but after a while it will stop. The equilibrium may be disturbed but it may be regained soon. There is a third kind of equilibrium. Place the pencil horizontally, e.g., lay it down on the table; it is at rest. In this position, wherever you place the pencil, it is at rest. *It is in equilibrium all the time.*

In like manner, there are some people whose minds are always disturbed and distracted. So they can hardly be in equilibrium or rest – external circumstances bring them to rest for a while but they are distracted again. The second category of people are those whose minds are usually calm, collected and quiet, but being disturbed once, they go on oscillating for a long time. The majority of us are like that.

You are walking down the lane; somebody comes and shakes hands with you and makes a critical remark to you. He goes away but the effect of his remark causes disequilibrium in your mind. The disturbance lingers on for hours, even for days and weeks. Your mind thus keeps on oscillating; being once disturbed it goes on oscillating, moving to and fro like the pendulum. This state of mind ruins your peace and your life.

If you could prevent these peculiar oscillations and overcome inner disturbances, your life could be peaceful and the mind would attain balance. Even 30 years of your life may be equivalent to a hundred. This disease of the mind must be known and cured – this disease of an oscillating mind makes most of us a *pendulum man.* We keep oscillating between a tear and a smile.

The third kind of people are heroes whose minds cannot be disturbed under any circumstances. Place them in the surfing waves of the rolling ocean, they are the same; place them in war, there is no difference. Even adverse remarks leave them unruffled. Their minds are as fresh as ever. Such a person is a liberated soul or a man of wisdom. You may come and praise him all the time; go away and his mind will not afterwards be dwelling on your praise. When criticised, he will not be ruminating over your criticisms. *Being free he believes in his Divinity and is of neutral equilibrium.*

Strive to be of the third kind. Free and engrossed in your divinity. If you study Vedanta and keep the Vedantic teachings continually before you, and by imbibing the essence of AUM you remember your Godhead and the reality, if your mind was originally of an unstable equilibrium, it will become of stable equilibrium, and if of stable equilibrium, it will acquire neutral equilibrium, says Swami Rama Tirtha.

OO

Would you opt for the road less travelled?

To know not oneself is suicide,
To kill oneself is love for things
That stand outside as non-self's forms;
To live, indeed, is life in God
Undivided in love of God,
To sequestration resorting,
Away from crowd and mob and noise,
Absorbed in pursuit of glorious aims;
He hails as greatest knower known,
Of him there is no peer in the world,
All faiths, all cults and religions
Do merge in this boundless sea.
–Bhagavad Gita XIII.28,10,11

As a human being, you are endowed with the seed of great divine potential. You are free to realise His Divine Self. Saints and seers have emerged, since time immemorial, from within humankind only: the Buddha, Guru Nanak, Swami Vivekananda, Ramana Maharshi and many more. You are made up of the same stuff as God. *"Mamai Vanshojeevloke Jeevbhoota Sanatana,"* says Lord Krishṇa to Arjuna in the 15th Chapter of the *Bhagavad Gita*, meaning thereby that "an element of Me is essentially present in all living beings". Thus you have an additional prerogative.

As a human being, you are free to educate yourself to live life meaningfully. It is *your* freedom to be blissful or miserable – to remain in darkness or to live a life of light.

This is your rare prerogative as a human being, says Osho. On the other hand, birds, animals, plants are destined to live as they are. But you have the option to become a saint or a devil. You have to choose *the road less travelled* – the road that Buddha chose, that Swami Rama Tirtha chose, that Swami Yogananda chose.

In a sense, you are truly liberated to carve your own destiny, to choose the righteous path in life or succumb to temptation – the short-lived pleasures of the world.

In making your choice, do not forget the basic truth of life that you cannot hold on to anything finite. And the one who enjoys happiness of the Self ceases to care for the ephemeral – the material worldly attractions.

OO

Can you take personal control of your life?

Are you anxious to reform the world? Then first see that you have reformed yourself, made yourself new, through communion and prayer and selfless work.

To trust God is to accept His Will in all conditions and circumstances of life. To trust Him is to rejoice in all that happens. In sickness and suffering, in calumny and ill will, in loss of possessions and power, in danger, disaster and death, let the heart sing: though He slay me, yet will I put my trust in Him.

When you accept Him as your ultimate anchor, an ethereal peace shall prevail upon your psyche strengthening it with an inner divine peace and stability of mind.

–JP Vaswani

Very often, you tend to take pride in your success and curse circumstances for your failure. You feel as though your circumstances and other people control you. A stranger on the street can abuse you and spoil your day. You live in fear about what your boss will do or say, and you base your life's goal on making your parents proud of you. Thus your reactions are based on *external* events. You tend to enslave yourself to your feelings, habits, thoughts, actions and reactions. Why is this? Vedanta and Buddhism have a word for these conditioned thoughts or deeds of man – *samskaras.* Your *samskaras* create the personality you possess.

How? Your mind is composed of two parts – the conscious and the subconscious. The subconscious is at the root of many of your thoughts and behaviour. You cannot control these consciously, which explains why you have difficulty losing some of your miserable habits that you wish to change, such as overcoming anger or kicking off the cigarette-smoking habit. But you can certainly master the art of changing them if you understand *how* they come into being.

The subconscious part of your mind is fully influenced by your thoughts. If you repeatedly programme it with positive and affirmative thoughts such as "I am worthwhile" and "likeable" and "good", the subconscious mind gets this message automatically and operates from these assumptions giving rise to behaviour which is *now* more open, spontaneous and likeable.

Thus, other people like you too in turn and transmit messages to say that you are "good" and "worthwhile" and this strengthens your original impression about yourself through positive thoughts. This is how you create your personality from your beliefs. This is also known as the self-fulfilling prophecy in psychological terminology – whereby you shape your personality through your belief system.

Your early parental treatment during the foundation years of early childhood, the early schooling, your peer group pressures and so on have propelled you to form an opinion about yourself, and you have come to *believe* it. If it is a negative image, you have to reshape it by de-conditioning your in-built negative image.

As Lord Buddha said: "We live in a mind-made world." Thoughts invade our mind like powerful volcanoes. It is for us to manage them through proper channelisation for self-growth.

OO

Desires

Desire is the cause of all misery.
If your desire remains unfulfilled,
it leads to frustration and causes misery.
If it does get fulfilled, it leaves you empty.
–Lord Buddha

The root cause of man's suffering lies in holding on to the pleasant and avoiding the unpleasant. No one wants to come out of one's comfort zone to embrace the tough, the unseen or the unpleasant. Man is stuck in the dualities of life - in the dichotomy of the pleasant and the unpleasant. The mind gets agitated if one is unable to achieve the desirable. But when a particular desire is fulfilled, another one raises its head and the vicious cycle goes on and on. Desires are endless.

You may have experienced that at several points of time in life you *really* believed that if a particular desire was fulfilled you would finally become happy and satisfied. But were you really contented thereafter? If yes, for how long? Soon, new desires overtook you without your realisation and you found yourself in the same situation all over again, chasing a new desire!

According to Vedanta, our happiness depends upon the number of desires reduced by us. Our happiness quotient is equivalent to the gap between the number of desires fulfilled, divided by the number of desires entertained.

$$\textbf{Happiness} = \frac{\text{Number of desires fulfilled}}{\text{Number of desires entertained}}$$

The gap between them decides our happiness. The smaller the gap, the more will be our happiness quotient. So, if we decrease the denominator, i.e., entertain less number of desires, or enter a state of no desire, it will automatically take care of our happiness quotient and ensure peace of mind. But if this is not so, it leads to frustration, depression, and even destructive elements amongst mankind.

Anger and aggression become the order of such an era. Today's era is such that every hand seems to hold a stone to attack the other's head! When God is omnipresent and omniscient, why do these meaningless religious conflicts occur on earth? And when Man knows his fate only too well, why does he nurture his great ego for status and power? Such a human scenario occurs due to the unenlightened lot, oblivious to the true values of realisation.

To conquer dualities of life, i.e., joy versus sorrow, pleasure versus pain etc, you must learn *to hold on to nothing and resist nothing.* Live like the lotus - unaffected by the muddy surroundings in which it grows. Be like the lotus-leaf - unaffected and unwetted by the drop of water on it.

Surprisingly, man seldom lives in the present moment, but wanders in the labyrinths of the past or the future - in a medley of regrets, despair, anger, worry, fear etc. Haunted by past failures, he is filled with apprehensions about the future. He thus views his whole life through this prism.

Make your mind like a calm lake. Attain poise by calming the mind's ever chattering and desire-filled nature. Realisation of the True Self requires stillness of mind as a prerequisite. You can attain it by becoming *antarmukhi* - looking inwards and not being distracted by external trivialities.

OO

Spirituality at work

In your daily spiritual practice,
be like the river that does not recognise any obstacle.
The very commitment is the driving force.
Don't wait for the right time.
Make a way for yourself if you cannot see one.
–Bapu Asaram

At our workplace, we work with people of different propensities. For this, we have to adjust with everybody. Unfortunately, most of us are not able to do so and, therefore, face problems arising out of ego clashes and professional jealousies. To transcend these negative emotions, we have to practise moral and spiritual values. All emotions are in the mind only. To transcend the negative qualities, you have to control the mind through discrimination. For example, anger can be controlled through pure love, miserliness through charity, jealousy through appreciation of talents and so on.

Conscious practice of certain moral and spiritual values in life becomes a habit and continuous habits mould character. Once these spiritual values become the character of a person, spiritual growth takes place and he commands honour and respect automatically.

Thanks to a few New Age gurus like Deepak Chopra, spirituality has today become an accepted corporate buzzword. To check whether or not you are stretching your spiritual dimension at the office to extract the maximum out of your career potential, answer this quiz on organisational behaviour.

Answer the following questions with 'Mostly', 'Sometimes' or 'Never':

Do you:

- ❖ Keep your cool, no matter what emergency arises at work?
- ❖ Never waste a single moment of your day?
- ❖ Never lament a mistake, knowing that "too much" regret is also wrong?
- ❖ Flow with your own nature and give the same freedom to your subordinates?
- ❖ Try to laugh at least once a day?
- ❖ Try to learn something from the wise and the stupid?
- ❖ Try to increase your attention span, despite pressing problems?
- ❖ Keep time free for yourself at least once a day?
- ❖ Try not to repress your emotions?
- ❖ Take failures in your stride?
- ❖ Act in the moment, thoughtfully and according to the situation?
- ❖ Mingle with others but without losing your self-identify?
- ❖ Suffer fools gladly?
- ❖ Come to ground zero at the end of each hectic day?
- ❖ Don't jump to conclusions while judging others?
- ❖ Find out what you wish to do and then just do it?
- ❖ Attempt to figure out the purpose of your life, even when there are no answers forthcoming?
- ❖ Turn to your inner island of tranquillity even in the midst of cacophony?
- ❖ Live in society but don't let society live in you?
- ❖ Live in a state of fearlessness?
- ❖ Immerse yourself fully in the immediate task?
- ❖ Have your own sense of reality, based on personal experiences?

- Realise that nothing happens by chance, everything happens by choice?
- Remember that to live life meaningfully, and fulfil your highest potential, you must first be honest with yourself?
- Realise that what you see is only part of the truth?
- Make yourself accountable for your own growth?

Scoring

Assign yourself two marks for 'Mostly', one mark for 'Sometimes' and zero for 'Never'.

Interpretation

A score between 35 and 52: Excellent.

Between 18 and 34: Fairly good.

Between 1 and 17: Poor.

OO

Do you keep your cup empty when praying?

The years roll on, one by one.... But I am still far from God. May I learn, more and more, to forget myself, to foresake myself, as forgetfulness of self is remembrance of God.

And I pray to thee O Lord, so bless me that in all the changing vicissitudes of life I may never lose sight of Thee. And make me, Divine Master, an instrument of Thy help and healing in this world of suffering and pain.

–TL Vaswani

When you worship, keep your cup of receptivity open and empty for the Lord's grace to fill it. If your cup is already full hoping for some particular gains or expectations, there will be no room for God's grace to fill your already full cup.

Have faith and believe that He knows what is best for you even without your asking. Says Sri Sri Ravi Shankar: "A bird when it flies high just floats. You have to float in life in full acceptance." And be grateful to Him for His gifts of life to you. The most unfortunate people are those who never feel grateful. Gratefulness itself fulfils the purpose of life. It brings joy and you experience fullness.

Feel the grace of God within your inner self, without giving words to it. As expressed meaningfully in these lines of Sri Sri Ravi Shankar:

In the very process of expressing the truth, the truth becomes untruth. In forming words, it is lost; whatever can be known, can be only in deep silence.... A thousand hours of speech cannot equal one glance, a hundred glances cannot equal one minute of silence.

So learn to meditate in silence. Silence is cessation of the mind. In it the 'other' disappears. Feel oneness with God by being quiet for a while.

And in that quietude, contemplate upon your true original Self – which is nothing but a significant spark of the ever effulgent, enlightened Supreme Power. Just as the Sun in its original self is extremely hot, yet when it is reflected in a dew drop, it acquires the properties of the cool dew drop, or when reflecting itself on an ice-cold lake, its reflected image too acquires the cold properties of the lake reflecting it, similarly, when God reflects Himself through Man, the original nature of God is changed according to the quality and individuality of the person. If he is a dull person, the reflected Godliness is dulled. If he is a spiritually evolved person, the quality of God's reflection in him gets visibly pronounced.

OO

The spiritual Guru

I bow to the Guru who is the cause
of (the existence of) all the worlds,
who enables one to cross the ocean
of the Universe (to attain liberation)
and who is the source of all knowledge and bliss.
I bow to the Guru on whose existence
depends the existence of the Universe,
whose effulgence illuminates it, and whose
bliss is at the root of Creation.
In spite of its diversity, the Universe is one.
Likewise the Guru (Brahma) and the
knowledge (Brahma Jnana)
He imparts are One. I salute the Guru in this form.
–Guru Gita (from Skand Puran 3.209)

For man Guru is Shiva, Guru is God,
Guru is the friend, Guru is the soul,
and Guru is the living being.
There is really nothing except the
Guru anywhere in this world.
–Skand Puran 2.85

If all the lights of your room suddenly went out, you would not be able to see where you and your belongings are. Everything would become obscure. Similarly, we are all immersed in the darkness of this material world. The material world is dark and needs sunlight or moonlight for illumination. However, there is another world, a spiritual world that is beyond darkness. That world is described by Lord Krishna in the *Bhagavad Gita* (15.6): "That abode of Mine is not illumined by the sun or the moon, nor by any other light. One who reaches it never returns to this material world."

When you wish to start your spiritual journey for this amazing spiritual abode, you need a Guru to guide you towards the right path. The Guru's objective is to take his disciples from darkness to light.

Presently, everyone is suffering due to ignorance, just as one contracts a disease out of ignorance. Just as a child will touch the fire, not knowing that the fire burns, and the fire does not think, 'This is a child and does not know I will burn', likewise there is no excuse for our ignorance. The Guru's task is to ensure that no human being suffers or is misled in the labyrinths of this material world.

You can suffer three kinds of miseries in this material world – those arising from: (a) material body and mind, (b) from other living entities (such as ants, mosquitoes, flies etc) and (c) from the forces of nature (earthquakes, famines, floods etc). All of us tend to suffer from any or all of them. No one can say that he is completely free from suffering. We suffer out of our ignorance. The Guru rescues his devotees from ignorance. We send our children to school to save them from suffering. If our children do not receive education, we fear they will suffer in the future.

The Guru realises that suffering is due to ignorance, which is akin to darkness. How can one in the darkness of ignorance be saved? By the light of wisdom! The Guru shows us the torchlight of knowledge and relieves us from being enveloped in darkness.

A Guru is absolutely necessary for the spiritual seeker. To understand spiritual life, God, proper action, and one's relationship with God, the Guru has to be worshipped like the Supreme Personality of Godhood. Complete surrender has to be there, for without surrender we cannot learn anything.

If we go to a Guru simply to challenge him, we will learn nothing. The Guru has to be accepted in all earnestness and faith, as Arjuna did when he accepted Lord Krishna as his Guru on the battlefield of Kurukshetra. The Guru should be offered the same respect as one offers God, as God accepts our surrender to the Guru as surrender to Himself. The Guru is addressed as *Prabhupada. Prabhu* denotes "Lord", and *pada* means "position". Thus *Prabhupada* means "he who has taken the position of the Lord".

In the *Bhagavad Gita* (4.34) Lord Krishna Himself tells us the method of seeking and approaching the Guru: "Just try to learn the truth by approaching a spiritual master. Enquire from him reverently and render service unto him. The self-realised soul can impart knowledge unto you because he has seen the truth."

But we should not accept a Guru immediately out of zeal. That is rather dangerous. We must first find a bona fide Guru, then establish our relationship with him, and act accordingly. This will lead to success and enlightenment in life, for one who engages in the spiritual activities of unalloyed devotional service at once transcends the modes of material nature and is elevated to the spiritual platform.

The Guru takes on the great responsibility of guiding his disciplines and enabling them to become eligible candidates for the perfect position of immortality – of no more birth, no more death, no more old age, no more disease.

The Guru must be competent to lead his disciple back home – back to Godhead. In a dialogue with Goddess Parvati, Lord Shiva says (*Skand Puran*, 1.27): "The devotion and worship of one's spiritual Master (Guru) is devotion and worship towards Me. When one contemplates on one's Guru, it is contemplation on Me. The word 'Gu' denotes darkness (ignorance) and 'Ru' means light (knowledge). So the one who dispels the darkness of ignorance and ignites his light of knowledge (of God realisation) is a Guru."

It is further stated in the 44th shloka of *Skand Puran*: "If Shiva gets offended by a devotee, the Guru can save him from God's wrath, but if a devotee offends his Gurudev, no one can save him."

Says Lord Shiva to Goddess Parvati (*Gurugeeta*): "Sceptical scientists, astrologers, workers for worldly pursuits, and the materialistic men are unaware of the purity and sanctity of the auric power of the Guru. The living entity reincarnates itself helplessly again and again like the revolving *rahat* (water-drawing revolving machine used in the fields) due to its darkness of ignorance. By shunning one's Guru, even a *yogi* cannot attain salvation. Without serving one's Guru even the *Gandharvas* (Gods of music), one's forefathers, *Yakshas*, saints, and gods cannot attain *Mukti* (salvation)."

The Lord continues: "Just as the insect who contemplates upon the black bee eventually becomes the black bee itself, so also a living being contemplating upon *Brahman* (the Almighty) attains divine characteristics. Always contemplating upon one's Guru, the living being undoubtedly turns divine, no matter where he dwells..." (*Skand Puran* 2.82,83)

According to the Vedas and ancient Hindu scriptures, worship of the spiritual Guru relieves one of his deadliest of sins. If one firmly shuns the company of the wicked and refrains from sinning, such inclinations of his heart and mind bestow upon him initiation by the Guru (*deeksha*). The Guru follows his devotee even when the devotee is on his deathbed. He accompanies his soul heavenwards and grants him peace and *moksha* even in his journey beyond this earthly planet.

OO

Why should you have a Guru?

In order to learn the transcendental sciences one must approach the bona fide spiritual master, who is fixed in the Absolute Truth.
–Mundaka Upanishad 1.2.12

You know that God has sent a spark of Him within you, which needs to be nurtured through constant awareness until you become it. Because you are spirit souls, you cannot be happy in the material atmosphere. It is like taking fish out of water. It cannot be happy without water. Similarly, if you are without spiritual consciousness, you can never be happy. The human body is an excellent vehicle by which we can reach eternal life. It is a rare and very important boat for crossing over the ocean of nescience or ignorance, which is material existence.

On this boat, there is the service of an expert boatman, the Guru or spiritual master. By divine grace, the boat plies the water in a favourable wind. If one neglects this goal, it is suicidal. Says Swami Prabhupada, founder of the International Society of Krishna Consciousness: "There is certainly a great deal of comfort in the first-class coach of a train, but if the train does not move towards its destination, what is the benefit of an air-conditioned compartment? Contemporary civilisation is much too concerned with making the material body comfortable. No one has information of the real destination of life, which is to go back to Godhead."

Hence just being seated in a comfortable compartment should not satisfy us. We must also see whether or not our vehicle is moving towards its real destination. The boat of human life is constructed in such a way that it must move towards a spiritual destination.

The Guru can enable one to achieve this goal. Taking on a Guru is not simply a fad. One who is serious about understanding spiritual life requires a Guru. Surrender must be there, for without surrender we cannot learn anything. We must accept the Guru as Arjuna accepted Sri Krishna Himself as his Guru. If we surrender to the bona fide guru, we surrender to God. God accepts our surrender to the Guru. When we offer respect to the Guru, we are offering respect to God. Because we are trying to be God-conscious, it is required that we learn how to offer respect to God through God's representative.

Because he is the most confidential servitor of God, the Guru is offered the same respect we offer God. We must carry out all his orders. In the *Bhagavad Gita* (4.34) Lord Krishna Himself tells us the method of seeking and approaching the Guru: "Just try to learn the truth by approaching the spiritual master. Inquire from him submissively and render service unto him. The self-realised soul can impart knowledge unto you because he has seen the truth."

The spiritual master is one who solves all the confusion of his devotees, as he has received the mercy of God, and he can deliver the solution to the confused man. If you are sincere, God sends you a spiritual master. Therefore God is also called *Chaityana-guru*, the spiritual master within the heart. God helps from within and without.

"The genuine Guru is God's representative and he speaks about God and nothing else.... A genuine Guru is not a businessman. Whatever God says, the Guru repeats. He does not speak otherwise," says Swami Prabhupada in an interview with the *London Times*. "If we send a telegram, the person who delivers the telegram does not have to correct it, edit it, or add to it. He simply presents it. That is the Guru's business. The Guru may be this person or that, but the message is the same; therefore it is said that the Guru is one."

In the *Srimad Bhagavatam* (11.17.27) the Blessed Lord says: "One should understand the spiritual master to be as good as I am. Nobody should be jealous of the spiritual master or think of him as an ordinary man, because the spiritual master is the sum total of all demi-gods." That is, the spiritual master has been identified with God Himself. He has nothing to do with the affairs of this mundane world. He appears before us to reveal the light of the *Vedas* and to bestow upon us the blessings of full-fledged freedom, for which we should yearn at every step of our life's journey.

The *Svetasvatara Upanishad* (6.23) reveals: "Only unto those great souls who simultaneously have implicit faith in both the Lord and the spiritual master are all the imports of Vedic knowledge automatically revealed."

OO

Service to Mankind

This body is the field of work,
Within it is the lord of deeds;
This master ensouling all fields
Is also the Universal Soul.
–Bhagavad Gita XIII.1,2

In the words of Sathya Sai Baba: "Human life is most precious, highly sacred, beautiful and invaluable. The body is an indispensable vehicle for experiences. Without it nothing can be done, not even a simple task. The human body is therefore more precious than worldly wealth and such other material acquisitions. By making proper use of the body, and engaging it in sacred actions, life must be sanctified."

Time gone by will never return again. Once the Ganges merges with the ocean, you cannot get back even a drop of its sacred water. Likewise, once life ebbs away and the body is gone, it cannot be recovered.

The human body is also a clock marking time and the passage of life. It ticks away the seconds, minutes, days, weeks, months and years. Man knows that life is ticking away and yet he does not bother to enquire about the real purpose of life. No one can say when the clock will stop. It is, therefore, most essential to make proper use of life while it is still available.

The body is the vehicle for the journey of life. If the vehicle is not properly maintained, one must be prepared to face serious problems on the way.

Your body has been gifted to you in order to serve others. You must firmly resolve not only to take care of yourself but of others also. Unfortunately, today man does not know what service means. The essence of all the 18 Puranas can be summarised in two short sentences: *Help ever. Hurt never.*

Though God has given the body for service, man does not seem to understand what help means, being ever immersed in selfish acts. Every thought, every word, and every action is driven by selfishness. Man has become a puppet in the hands of self-interest. How can a puppet ever be called independent? Selfishness must therefore be totally rejected and selflessness must be wholeheartedly embraced. Then alone would the real purpose of the human body and human life be realised.

You must make an effort to realise that your body is just an instrument given to you for a specific purpose and you must also understand that purpose. The body must be used only for performing good deeds. You must lead a virtuous life. In the end, you must give up the body with good thoughts. Do not assume that the body has been given for enjoyment, seeking comfort, beautification and useless pursuits of like nature. Indulgence in pleasure seeking, comfort and luxury can be dangerous. God has not given this body for indulgence.

Safeguard your body by all means and take full care of your health, but use your body solely to perform good acts.

Harmony in Nature

The stirring of a flower on earth troubles a distant star.... as everything in the universe is in dynamic interaction.
–Osho

When a pebble is thrown into a pond, the waves so produced affect the entire pond's water. Likewise, all movements, all activities of living beings and men create vibrations in the atmosphere. By their expansion in the atmosphere, they spread in the entire universe, since the whole universe is one unit and all forms are part of the whole.

In this holistic approach man, animal, and Nature are considered interrelated and interdependent. Thus the effect of an act performed by any being does not remain with the doer but affects the entire universe. What acts of which being are useful or harmful to the universe is beyond the discretion of man.

Man with his limited knowledge is not aware of the entire universe and the numerous *karmas* of innumerable living species. To what extent an act favourably or unfavourably affects other beings is beyond the comprehension of man. The favourable and unfavourable effects of man's actions and all sub-human species can only be decided by the Omniscient, who is the creator of the universe, who has also created all *karmas* and their fruits. Only the Almighty Creator can enlighten us about the favourable and unfavourable effects of actions.

Humanity's deviations from His Law of Life create imbalances and disruptions in the harmonious operations of the universe, which lead to incarnation of the Lord in this universe to restore balance, as stated in the *Sanatana Dharma.*

The law of laws is eternal harmony. A strict adherence to the Divine Law is desirable for perfect harmony and balance in creation. No one has any right to disturb the balance of Nature. If an individual attempts to move in a direction other than that in which Nature is moving, the individual is sure to be crushed sooner or later by the enormous pressure of the opposing force.

The whole universe is beautiful because of its divine harmony, order, rhythm and balance and the divinity of the cosmos can only be perceived on stepping out of self-interest. As Sri Asaram contends in his discourses: "Today, man with his one hand over the gun aspires to be affluent and attain happiness from violence. But since times immemorial, it is only too apparent that the human race can never derive happiness from violence. By bomb blasts and manipulations, man can only create imbalance in the cosmos."

On the contrary, empathy, compassion, and altruism are the dire need of the hour. This is the only path for global peace, harmony and happiness on earth.

Can you cope with destructive criticism?

I love those who criticise me – as they are my teachers in my path of self-growth.
–Swami Vivekananda

When faced with envy and futile mudslinging, be calm and unconcerned. "Do not damage your health by anger or worry. Be happy, on the other hand," says Sathya Sai Baba. "Bhasṃasura – who won from Shiva the power of causing a conflagration on the body of anyone upon whose head he placed his hand – tried to kill Shiva Himself by his newly won capability; but God so manipulated events that, unaware of what he was doing to himself, Bhasmasura was tempted to place his hand upon his own head; he thus died in the conflagration that he lit upon himself. So too those in wickedness and pride will be reduced to ashes in the fire of repentance."

In fact, a gentleman who ignorantly equated Baba with his own species of exhibitionistic yogis and challenged him to do a much-advertised feat was humiliated by his own conceit and his promoters suffered dramatic discomfiture.

Baba analysed the motives of these men afflicted with pride. Baba said: "Egoism is the seed-plot of a host of dragging tendencies like greed, anger, malice and hate. It clouds the intelligence and distorts the face of the real into disgusting features of the false. It hides truth in a cloud of dust and urges man into immoral deeds in the effort to cater to the claims of self-aggrandisement."

Like Baba, forgive your critics, for they are, in Baba's words: "Moths whose nature is to bore into fabrics. They cannot but do anything else; they have an inner impulse, which they have not been taught to overcome. The moth bores into cotton saris, woolen clothes, silk vestments; it has no discrimination in its make-up." So be happy that they are deriving joy by reviling you. Your aim is to render all men joyful. If these men can derive joy through such means, why should *you* deny them that avenue for the expression of their nature?

"Pray for their transformation," Baba continues, "into Sattvic individuals, for the speedy cure of their blindness, for their tongues to recognise the taste of truth. Direct your love to these misguided brothers; they will rejoin the pilgrim path soon."

OO

Is compassion a way of life with you?

It is of the Lord's mercies that we are not consumed, because His compassions fail not. They are new every morning.
–Lam 3.22-23

Does your soul lend its ear to every cry of pain? "Let not the fierce Sun dry one tear of pain before you have wiped it off from the sufferer's eye. But let each burning human tear drop on thy heart and there remain, nor even brush it off, until the pain that caused it is removed," says HP Blavatsky, the author of *The Voice of the Silence.*

When we are bound to another human being in triumph and disaster, we are lifted above the passion of pity and envy; his grief is our grief; his joy is our joy; we are as one in a union of hearts.

We must aim only at striving to channel better the love power of the universe, so that we may add to the sum total of happiness in this world and "try to lift a little of the heavy *karma* of the world", says Clara Codd, the author of *The Ageless Wisdom of Life.*

We can call ourselves humane only when we learn to *feel with* others, as compassionate beings. It is the crown of consciousness marking the king among men; but it is a crown that any commoner may lift to his own head. That crown does not signify conquest or power over others, but conquest and power over the self.

The degree to which you are sensitive to other people's suffering, to other men's humanity, is the index of your own humanity.

We know that God pervades all living beings. Then why is it that some men catch animals, tie them mercilessly with ropes and slaughter them with the butcher's knife by beheading? Is it not ruthless?

Saint Kabir reveals the bitter truth and ponders over the Mohammedan custom of *vaju* (washing of hands, face and feet) before offering *sajda* to God inside the mosque. He asked the *maulvis* (clergy) what the purpose was in praying five times a day and repeatedly saying that God is one and dwells in everybody but then hurting God's living creatures outside the mosque just for their taste. If a man does not purify his mind, reciting God's name for the entire day is of no use.

It is said that man achieves fullness of being in fellowship and the care of others. The degree of our being human stands in the degree to which we care for others. Help others and you shall be helped yourself, in virtue of the never failing and ever active Law of Compassion.

Understand yourself and your place in the universe. In the words of Guru Maa Anandmurti: "If you are kind to animals, God will be kind to you. Every person has a right to live and no one wishes to die. Likewise, animals also do not like to be killed. They also like to live like man. Christ also said that God would be kind to them only when they are kind to others. If you snatch others' right to live how can you claim your own right to live?"

She further asserts that biologically too, man's teeth and intestines are not made to tear and eat the flesh of animals. Unlike flesh-eating non-vegetarian animals that possess long, pointed teeth, man has even teeth. Herbivorous animals like the cow, horse, goat, donkey and buffalo also possess even, broad teeth. Thus, there is no doubt that nature wants man to be vegetarian and has bestowed him the structure of teeth and intestines like that of vegetarian animals.

It is said that you are what you eat. If that is so, think of the fear and terror ingrained in the animal's psyche when it is slaughtered; the anger, hatred and fear at that juncture brings about certain chemical changes in the animal's flesh. Science has proved that the effect of these negative emotions goes into your blood when you eat that poisonous and toxic flesh, and it has the some negative influence on your psyche. You turn *tamasic.*

Thousands of pilgrimages and fasts are worthless in seeking God if one is addicted to liquor and meat-eating habits. In the eyes of God, taking the life of any creature is the most heinous crime. Such killers will be surely punished by God. Just for taste if someone kills a goat or chicken, the killer will also be killed in the same manner, according to the theory of *karma.*

All our saints and scriptures emphasise that bread earned by sincere and honest efforts makes the person eating it an honest human being. This also holds true for your children and you. Please give them honestly earned bread so that they become sincere and honest. It is for this reason that Guru Nanak preferred Bhai Lala's simple bread to Malik Bhaga's delicacies. He further says that he only relishes the simple bread offered with love. Love begets love. It is true between two human beings as also in the behaviour of God.

In one of his past life stories, Lord Buddha relates how a pandit took a goat to be sacrificed before Goddess Kali. The pandit smeared *sindoor* (holy red powder) on the goat's forehead and garlanded the goat, as it was customary for pandits to observe these rituals before the sacrifice of any animals before a Godhead or Goddess. When the goat was about to be slaughtered, a strange thing happened. The goat laughed and then wept loudly. The pandit was amazed and asked the goat the reason for laughing, then weeping.

The goat narrated her story. She said that she had been in the cycle of 500 rebirths as a goat. This was the last cycle. She would then be reborn as a human. She had been a pandit in a previous birth and had slaughtered a goat. As a consequence, she was punished with 500 rebirths as a goat. With her killing by the pandit, she would be saved and become human. Her being slaughtered is a sign of her happiness. She then added that she was feeling aggrieved because of the pandit's fate. He might receive 500 rebirths in the form of a goat as punishment.

The pandit was touched by the story and realised his folly, bowed his head before the goat and thanked her for saving him from the wrath of God. He had decided not to sacrifice the goat before the Goddess. The goat was however keen to receive a human birth. The pandit untied the rope and set her free. The story continues that on seeing the goat, a greedy man tried to catch her but she ran away and fell into a valley, thus ending her cycle of animal life.

In the *Gurbani* too, one finds a good description about the importance of human births. As stated in Sikh, Buddhist and Hindu scriptures, we receive human birth after a succession of animal rebirths – as elephants, fish, deer, lion or insects. This is after a great deal of effort and by the grace of God, as stated in the *Gurbani*: *Kai janam bhaye keet – patanga, kai janam gaj meen kuranga.*

Some people argue that by not consuming meat the population of goats, hens and other creatures will increase and thus, eating them balances animal populations. But have they ever thought that the population of humans is also increasing alarmingly, especially in India, China, Pakistan and South Asia. The governments of these countries are concerned and taking necessary measures to check it. Unemployment and poverty is also growing in these countries. But will these people undertake the noble cause of "balancing" the human population by eating human flesh? In some parts of the world the custom of cannibalism does exist, but we still wouldn't advocate such a solution!

Then why should we entangle ourselves in the throat-cutting cycle with animals? We should consume food that generates pure thoughts. Eating animal flesh is not healthy as you sometimes eat the meat of animals that are sick and diseased. The eating of diseased animal flesh caused the recent SARS outbreak in China and other parts of the world. Some animals have made man suffer by transmitting various diseases. These viruses are difficult to tackle, as they are resistant to current medical treatments.

As children of God, we too need to do some soul searching and rethink this important issue and vow to God in our prayers that we will become vegetarians and teetotalers. In this way, if we can make a new beginning in our spiritual life, God will give us the strength to be worthy of our human life and seek salvation.

OO

Is your education really complete?

Our traditional Gurukul system of education used to instil spiritual knowledge in a student right from the age of five years onwards, and by the age of fifteen, sanctified values were inculcated in him which nurtured and awakened amazing Godly qualities and power in him. Such an education is a must and the need of the hour for our survival today.

–Bapu Asaram

In the era of stress, strife and violence, do we even pause for a moment and contemplate about what the real problem of our lives is? Our modern education is unequipped to give enlightenment about the real problem of life.

"The education system has degenerated into a course of training for mere living, not for reaching the goal of life," says Sathya Sai Baba. "It teaches skills and confers scholarships, but it does not concern itself with the resources latent in the deeper levels of consciousness, the springs of sympathy, service and renunciation, the urge to return to the heaven of joy from which one has come away. Man is being influenced by mass hysteria in all countries, so that he is becoming hard at heart, wooden in intelligence, and mechanical in mind."

Students must be taught disciplines that will enable them to tackle the stresses of life and overcome the inner adversaries of lust, greed, malice and hate.

Those who are educated and advanced in material knowledge scarcely introspect or ponder over the basic phenomena of birth, death, old age and disease. When one is physically diseased, he thinks the cure lies in a check-up with the physician. But he rarely bothers to get at the root of the disease. He never bothers to make a mental inquiry, "I did not *want* this disease. Why is this disease here then? Is it not possible to become free from disease?" He hardly ever thinks this way. This is because his intelligence is rather low. If an animal is brought to the slaughterhouse and sees another animal before him being slaughtered, he will still stand there grazing away merrily. He does not think his turn is next for being slaughtered!

When Yudhishthir was asked by Yamaraja, "What is the most surprising thing in this world?" Yudhishthir replied, "The most surprising thing is that every moment man sees his friends, his fathers and his relatives dying, but he still behaves as though death shall never touch him." Man never thinks that he will die, just as an animal never thinks that the next moment he may be slaughtered. It is satisfied with its grass. Similarly, man is satisfied with sense gratification. He does not realise that he too will die.

Just think for a while: "My father has died, my mother has died. So I will also have to die. Then what lies after death?" The *Bhagavad Gita* indicates that this knowledge is real education. The real inquiry is to question why we die at all. We do not want to become old, then why does old age come upon us?

To solve this problem, Chaitanya Mahaprabhu prescribed the chanting of the 'Hare Krishna' Mahamantra. With the chanting of God's name sincerely, the heart is cleansed and one can at once feel a transcendental ecstasy overpowering one's psyche. The blazing fire of our problematic material existence is extinguished. An ethereal realisation dawns upon us that *we do not belong to this material world.*

It is a folly to identify with this material world. Because people identify with this world, they think: "I am an Indian", "I am an American", and so on. But contemplation upon God's name makes one realise that he is not the material body. A voice seems to speak from deep within: "I do not belong to this material body or this material world. I am a soul, part and parcel of the Supreme. I am eternally related to Him and I have nothing to do with the material world." This is called *Brahma Jnana* – enlightened wisdom.

A person with this realisation has no duty to perform. Because we now identify our existence with this material world, we have many duties and debts. As quoted by Lord Krishna, Sanskrit literature recommends: "If one takes shelter with Me then he doesn't have to take the shelter of anyone else." So placing your love in God will ultimately make you happy. One may call God Allah, Krishna, Christ or something else, but simply place love in God. Learn to love God. That should be your only mission in this lifetime.

Do you suffer death anxiety?

The soul discards redundant forms
As one abandons worn-out clothes
For improved conditions ahead
In search of freedom bodiless.
–Bhagavad Gita II.22

"In each human body the two principles of immortality and death are established. By the pursuit of delusion, we reach death; by the pursuit of Truth, we attain immortality," says the *Mahabharata.*

Remember always that your original form as the *Atman* or your Supreme Soul is essentially a part of all-pervasive God. Since ages, your spirit or soul has been separated from God. It has already lived thousands of lifetimes on this planet. God in the form of the Life Force is present in all living beings. God is performing all actions and works according to *karmas,* subject to which the soul has come into a body.

In the form of the Life Force, God remains in a body so long as the *karmas* have to be done from that body. When the *karmas* of the soul are completed, the Life Force leaves the body and it falls to the ground. Through past-life regression therapy in their intensive psycho-pathological studies, psychiatrists have found that past-life traumas hold the key to most of our daily fears and phobias during the present lifetime.

Psychiatrist Dr Brian Weiss from Miami, Florida had been working with Catherine, a young patient suffering from recurrent nightmares and chronic anxiety attacks. Dr Weiss used hypnosis on her and was astonished when Catherine began recalling past-life traumas that proved ultimately to be the root cause of her insecurities and anxieties. Acting as a channel for information from highly evolved spirit entities called the 'Masters', Catherine revealed many secrets of life and death. This fascinating case is vividly mentioned in Dr Weiss' book, *Many Lives, Many Masters.* It opens up new vistas of scientific information on the mysteries of the mind, the continuation of life after death and the inevitable influence of our past-life experiences on our present behaviour.

The moment you realise that from pre-historic cave times to modern times, through innumerable lifetimes your in-dwelling spirit is eternal and undying and that the supreme goal of human life is not fulfilment of material desires but God-realisation and the moment you stop identifying with your physical body, the layers of conditional neurotic fears and anxieties, including death anxiety, shall be stripped away. With this genuine realisation, week-by-week you shall appear more and more serene, softer, loving and patient. You shall realise that death is nothing but a state of renewal.

Says Lord Krishna to Arjuna in his second discourse on Samkhya Yoga in the *Bhagavad Gita*: "Just as a man casts off worn-out clothes and puts on new ones, so also the embodied Self casts off worn-out bodies and enters others which are new."

Life is eternal; so we never die. In fact, we were never really born. Such a realisation dissolves the fear of death once and for all. Just imagine, if you knew you had lived countless times before and would live countless times again, how reassured you would feel. If you knew that well-wishing spirits were around to help you while you were in the physical state and that after death in the spiritual state you would rejoin these spirits, including your deceased loved ones, how comforted you would be.

If you knew that guardian angels really *did* exist, how much safer you would feel. If you knew that acts of violence and injustices against people did not go unnoticed, but had to be repaid in kind in other lifetimes, how much less anger and desire for vengeance you would harbour. And if by knowledge we indeed approach God, of what use are material possessions or power?

Most people recite prayers in churches, synagogues, mosques or temples – prayers that proclaim the immortality of the soul. Yet, interestingly, after their worship is over, they return to their competitive ruts, practising greed, manipulation and self-centredness. Little do they realise that these traits retard the progress of the soul.

But as you gradually *accept* and believe this truth, life becomes simple and more satisfying. There will be no need to play games, pretend, act out roles or be other than what you are. Relationships would become more honest and direct. Family life would be less confusing and more relaxed.

Many people in their very private experiences of paranormal events – extrasensory perception, precognition, out-of-body experiences, past-life dreams and the like – refrain from sharing their experiences with others. People are almost always afraid that by doing so others, including their own relatives, friends, and therapists, would consider them unstable. Yet these paranormal events are much more frequent and verified than people realise. It is only the reluctance to speak to others about these psychic occurrences that make them seem rare. Strangely enough, the highly trained are the most reluctant to disclose such experiences.

There's the case of the respected chairman of a major clinical department who was admired internationally. He spoke about the spirit of his deceased father, who protected him from serious danger several times. Another professor had dreams that provided the missing steps to his complex research experiments. The dreams, invariably, were correct and provided insights to him. Another well-known doctor usually knew who was calling him on phone before he even answered it.

Likewise, the wife of the chairman of psychiatry at a mid-western American university had a PhD in psychology. Her research projects were always carefully planned and executed. She had never told anyone that when she first visited Rome, she moved through the city as if she had a roadmap imprinted in her memory. She unerringly knew what was around the next corner. Although she had never been to Italy previously and did not know the language, Italians repeatedly approached her speaking in Italian, continually mistaking her for a native!

Thus, though highly trained professionals cannot deny their own experiences, yet their training being in many ways diametrically opposed to their information, personal experiences and beliefs accumulated over a period of time, they had chosen to remain quiet.

Nevertheless, their silence could not refute the basic truth experienced by them and researched by paranormal scientists that a part of us lives on even after death. And if that is so as documented in the sacred *Bhagavad Gita* through Lord Krishna's discourse to Arjuna, where is the cause to fear death? Says the blessed Lord Krishna to Arjuna (Chapter VIII.5,6): "Whosoever, leaving the body goes forth remembering Me alone at the time of death, he attains My Being. Whosoever at the end leaves the body thinking of any being, to that being only does he go, O Arjuna, because of his constant thoughts of that being. Therefore, at all times, remember Me only and fight. With the mind and intellect absorbed and fixed in Me, then shalt thou doubtlessly come to Me alone."

Is there any cause for fearing death, then?

OO

The homecoming

An American soldier killed on the field of battle in World War II, and discovered by a stretcher-bearer, wrote the following verses on the back of a cigarette box. The words:

Look God, I have never spoken to you,
But now I want to say "How do you do?"
You see God, they told me You didn't exist,
And like a fool, I believed all this.

Last night from a shell hole I saw your sky,
I figured right then they told me a lie.
Had I taken the time to see things You made,
I'd have known they weren't calling a spade a spade.

I wonder God if you'd shake my hand.
Somehow I feel You would understand.
Funny I had to come to this hellish place,
Before I had time to see Your face.

Well I guess there isn't very much more to say,
But I'm glad God I met you today.
I guess the 'Zero Hour' will soon be here.
But I'm not afraid since I know you are near.

The signal, well, God, I'll have to go;
I like you lots; and I want You to know,
Look, now this will be a horrible fight,

Who knows? I may come to Your home tonight;
Though I wasn't friendly to You before,
I wonder God if You'll wait at Your door.

I wish I had known You all these years.
Well, I have to go now, God; goodbye;
Strange – since I met you,
I'm not afraid to die....

OO

If I can

If I can throw a single ray of light,
Across the darkened pathway of another
If I can aid some soul to clear sight
Of light and duty and thus bless my brother
If I can wipe from any human cheek a tear
I shall not have, then, lived in vain while here.

If I can guide some erring to truth
Inspire within his heart a sense of duty,
If I can plant within the soul of a rosy plant
A sense of light, a love of truth and beauty;
If I can teach one man that God and Heaven are near,
I shall not have then lived in vain while here.

If from my mind I can banish the doubt and fear
And keep my life attuned to truth, love and kindness,
If I can scatter light and hope and cheer
And help and remove the curse of mental blindness,
If I can make joy more, more hope, less pain
I shall not have lived in vain while here.

If by life's roadside I can plant a tree
Beneath whose shade some wearied head may rest,
Though I may never share its shade or see
Its beauty I shall yet be truly blessed
Though no one knows my name.

–Anonymous

OO